Katrina Diary

WHAT THEY NEVER TOLD YOU ABOUT HURRICANE KATRINA

WRITTEN BY: *Ivy Stone*

This is a work of non-fiction and represents the true accounts of the aftermath of Hurricane Katrina.

Copyright © 2016 by Ivy Stone
ISBN: 978-0-692-62308-4

All rights reserved. No part of this publication may be reproduced, distributed, or transmitted in any form or by any means, including photocopying, recording, or other electronic or mechanical methods, without the prior written permission of the publisher, except in the case of brief quotations embodied in critical reviews and certain other noncommercial uses permitted by copyright law. For permission requests, write to the publisher, at the email address below:

ivystonepublishing@gmail.com

First Printing / January 2016

Published by: Ivy Stone Publishing, Michigan
Cover Design by: Wayne Ten II of TenSide Films, Michigan
Cover Formatting by: Casey Harris, Michigan

Quantity sales. Special discounts are available on quantity purchases by corporations, associations, and others. For details, contact the publisher at ivystonepublishing@gmail.com.

Or you may contact CreateSpace.com, Amazon.com or Barnes & Noble for any wholesale purchases.

Printed in the United States of America

DEDICATION

I dedicate this book to several of the most important people in my life.

To my father, John, who made this journey possible and who taught me the most important life lesson, to live for others. For showing me how to love and that loving others was the only way to become the best version of ourselves. For supporting my dreams, and for always being there for me in ways I could only hope one day to be there for others in the same capacity.

To my mother, Cheryl, for her support and assistance with editing this manuscript. For always making me laugh, and dreaming along with me on how we could change the world together. For always having the perfect answer to every problem and for teaching me strength, and how to be so strong that even if I was all by myself in any situation, that it would be enough.

To Ruby Rose and Spice Seraphina, my two pugs, for their constant love and affection and always making me feel like the most important person in the world to them. ☺

To Monica & Steve Glabach and their daughter Stacy for welcoming me into their family and treating me as one of their own with such love and support, I wouldn't be here today without their generosity.

To Joy Calloway for changing my life with her support and backing for my Medical Spanish Program for Healthcare Professionals that I developed. For believing in me and supporting my dreams.

To Laurie Jensen for her belief in me, and my passion to help others. For bringing my Medical Spanish Program into their hospital network and not only changing my life, but all of the patients we were able to help in turn with this educational resource.

To Dr. Joseph Abbate and his daughter Andrea Abbate for their extreme selflessness that truly impacted my life. For their love and belief in giving to others and living it. May God always bless them.

To Steve Pooley for his faithful support of mutual business endeavors and most importantly for his long-lasting friendship to my family and I. Thank you so much.

To Jordon Krain for his loyalty and friendship when I was traveling and truly saving my hide in quite sticky circumstances. Thank you, truly. I will always be grateful and indebted to you.

To Rondy Burgett for his loyal support for all my dreams, endeavors, acting and music hobbies. For his care and genuine love for my dogs and all the puppies that came along the way. I will always be grateful and pray that God will always bless you for your kindness.

To Scott Chestnut for his extreme hospitality, genuine friendship, and never-ending support for my dreams.

ACKNOWLEDGEMENT

Katrina Diary was written in the months following Hurricane Katrina at the end of 2005 and into the next year, 2006. The manuscript was completed shortly into the spring of 2006 and was suddenly lost when the laptop it was saved on crashed. Everything was lost.

Miraculously, in the summer of 2015 a hard copy of the Katrina Diary manuscript surfaced and was promptly re-typed and edited for publishing. It is truly a miracle that this book was recovered and was subsequently published. I am so grateful that God allowed for this miracle to happen, and to be able to finally share these never before heard stories, historical moments of Hurricane Katrina, and most importantly, a chance to inspire all, with these pages.

Please note that the quality of the pictures may not be as originally intended, since the digital copies were lost. The only copies that were recovered had to be scanned in. Thank you for understanding. (All photos were taken by the author, who owns the rights.)

I would like to express my sincere thanks to the American Red Cross for training me to volunteer on this Operation and for providing this special opportunity for me to share my time and heart to help the victims of Hurricane Katrina. I am so grateful that they believed in me at such a young age, (21 years old) to be capable and of value on such a large and vital recovery operation. Thank you from the bottom of my heart.

It truly doesn't matter your age or your skills, you can always reach out and help someone else. You are completely capable as God made you, to make a difference in your life, or the lives of others.

DISCLAIMER

The following pages are the true accounts of my experiences doing relief work on the Hurricane Katrina operation in Louisiana.

They are the stories that you didn't hear on the News, and they are memories that I will never forget.

I was assisting several different entities, including the American Red Cross. The book in its entirety is in reference to my 2005 deployment with the Red Cross.

It should be noted that nothing is meant to incriminate or associate directly with the privacy or independence of the entities or persons mentioned. The names of the characters have been changed to respect their privacy.

This diary is strictly from my perspective of the aftermath of Katrina and from the true accounts of my experiences on the frontlines of the operation, bringing to you, and to America, a true story.

-Rose

PURPOSE

I write this book as a testimony to America. The sole intent is to open the eyes of the public to the reality of how the News can be ingrained in our minds and memories as happenstance, incidences of chance, tragedies, or simple sad occurrences.

I seek to demonstrate how being disassociated by location can prohibit us from truly feeling or understanding those tragedies which may not directly affect us, several hundred miles away may be the very death of someone else.

Furthermore, this book has been written to prove that to truly make a difference in the life of someone else, you actually have act upon what you feel inside, something more than what is already being done.

Lastly, to show that despite all odds, one person, standing alone, has the power to change the world around them.

NOTE FROM THE AUTHOR:

Our lives are constantly filled with ups and downs. Many seek happiness and never find it. Happiness is found within our hearts, a gratitude for all things present. Being happy is to know that there is nothing that stands in the way of all of our dreams. It is something to fight for, to believe in, and to live for. Hold this passion inside of you, live it, and breathe it and all that you desire will come to life.

I hope the following pages will touch your heart in a way that will inspire and encourage you to follow your dreams and do whatever it takes to make them a reality in your own life.

Yours truly,

Rose

THE BEGINNING

WEDNESDAY, AUGUST 31, 2005
MY BIRTHDAY
10:59 A.M.

I frowned as I glanced at the clock. It was currently the exact time that I was born, twenty-one years prior. 10:59 a.m. Most kids my age were ecstatic on this day because it was the first time they could order a beer themselves. For me, I felt an impending sense of doom that I was aging way too fast. It sounds silly and stupid, but when you are known by those around you as the most ambitious girl alive, you realize that time is truly of the essence and each moment counts.

If life was simply meant to be lived out, it would almost seem too simple and completely meaningless. If we were meant to live out certain expectations how could anything in the world ever change? I wouldn't be required to do anything different than anyone else my age. I would go to college, get married, buy a minivan, have four kids, go to soccer games, grow old with them, and end up being a stay at home mom. *Me? No way! That would never work!* That piece of the puzzle didn't fit into the picture of my life.

Life wasn't simply a process for me; no, life to me was meant to be made, not just lived. It seems to be one of the hardest feats for mankind to accomplish with the pressure of having to look good, have money, nice things and have some sort of social status in day-to-day life. It turns into a life devoid of passion and one of simple existence.

I grabbed my cup of coffee drowned in milk, a little trick I'd learned in Costa Rica, and leaned back on the leather sofa to watch the news. I pulled a warm blanket close around me and blinked my eyes trying to adjust to the sunlight pouring in from the windows. I was feeling lazy and still sleepy from my peaceful night of rest. I decided to turn on the T.V. because I was curious to watch the television coverage for the new hurricane everyone was talking about. I had been so busy with work and sick from a recent bout of strep-pneumonia that I hadn't had a spare moment to tune into the latest news.

I turned to CNN and leaned back, sipping my steaming coffee. It has been termed as the beverage of the Gods and was my typical breakfast. I turned the volume up as I saw the newscaster come on. I paused for a moment, holding the coffee cup in mid-air as the devastating details of Hurricane Katrina started to come to life. Horrific images flashed upon the screen, and scenes of struggling survivors stole the moments. I saw victims clinging to trees as the cold water swirled around their feet threatening to drown them, rows of houses crushed by giant trees, power lines strewn all over the roadside and animals swimming in water with no sanctuary nearby to rest on. I watched intently for several minutes listening to every detail.

The thoughts of my birthday drifted away and a deep sadness swept over me. *How horrible!* I thought sadly as the news coverage sank in. I didn't watch too much more and was surprised that after a mere ten minutes I decided that I had seen enough. I quickly reached up and flipped off the T.V.

It was in those next few moments I felt my thoughts jumble up and a very disconcerting feeling take over. It didn't make sense to me to watch all these heart-wrenching details of how torn up the Southern part of the country was because of the wrath of Katrina. It was very sad and tragic but there was nothing I could do about it. I felt that by watching the hurricane coverage I was becoming depressed. I felt pity for the people that were suffering and pain to see so many lose their entire lives over such a quick and violent natural disaster.

Up in Michigan we weren't affected at all and still had our homes, jobs, money, family and friends. These people now had nothing. It made me really sad and I felt something tug at my heart wishing I could do something to help. It was a strange thought because I was just a young girl and didn't have anything to offer. I had no money, time, or anything that could possibly change the loss that these unfortunate victims now had to live with…forever.

I just sat there deep in thought thinking of all the millions of other people watching the same television coverage of the hurricane, some I'm sure with tears in their eyes. It just didn't make sense. Many of us would now donate money and goods to help the victims because we felt sorry for them.

I almost felt a little angry. It was almost a tragedy in itself that people didn't want to help someone else on just a normal day too. Why did it have to take such a horrible hurricane to get people to give back? Why? Why are we so proud that we pretend that bad things don't happen everyday? Why do we attempt to live our privileged lives close-minded to the fact that someone could always use our support, time or love?

With these thoughts in mind I just sat there and stared at the blank television screen. I wanted to help, but I certainly couldn't in any way and I didn't want to watch these people suffer anymore. I didn't want to even entertain the thought that I could drop my life here and just hop on a plane and assist in the relief efforts. I had a job and was currently spearheading a very important election for the local government office. I was barely twenty-one years old and had many bills to pay. I couldn't go without work! I had just finished college and I was busy. I had many things to do, places to go and people to see.

I was way too young to be involved with anything so far away from home and so catastrophic. I had no money to give and the only thing I could give was time and I didn't even have that. It wasn't even worth thinking about. I told myself that despite the desire to put my hands to work, it was not worth getting my hopes up. I pushed it out of my mind.

I got ready for work, took a quick warm shower and ate a small lunch. I almost felt guilty doing these things knowing that thousands were homeless down South and many of the victims struggling to survive were dying as the moments slipped by. The time passed, and later that afternoon, I sat down to study some Arabic and Russian before I got ready to go out in the evening to celebrate my birthday with a few close friends of mine.

The next morning I couldn't shake this uncomfortable feeling that I was being selfish. I knew that I wanted to help the victims and I felt that I could be of more assistance down there than I could be of any use up here. I had a great job, a home, a brand-new car and a safe, secure life. My life was full of happiness and good things, but it chagrined me to think that I could sit back and watch others suffer and do nothing about it. Bad things never seem to happen at a good time. They certainly always seem to happen at the wrong time. I wasn't used to dealing with this unsettling frame of mind, so I finally stopped for a moment to think about it all. I began to wrack my brain for ways that I could possibly do something, even something small to show my support for the victims.

After much pondering and many disappointing findings, I was left with one possibility. It was with this small glimmer of hope that I went to my father. I sat down with him discussing my wish to help with the relief efforts and then began explaining the factors that I was up against that were preventing me from doing it. He listened with concerned eyes and an understanding smile and shocked me with this reply.

He said, "Rose *if* the Red Cross needs you and ends up deploying you on the operation then I will take care of everything." He paused watching for my reaction.

A gigantic smile spread across my face and I quickly reached up and gave him a huge hug. My arms wrapped around him tightly and I held him for a few brief moments thinking how lucky I was to have such a caring father.

"I know you, and you have always wanted to help others. I think this will be good for you. You have a very giving heart."

It was in that moment I began to feel for the first time a realization of my desire. I began to actually believe that I was going to be able to do something for the first time in my life for someone else and not myself. It was an awesome feeling.

It seemed to be a miracle for sure but also one that I believe God allowed to happen, for the tales that I am about to share are tales that will be told from generation to generation and will forever be thread into the tapestry of America's history. They will leave a lasting impression of how one little girl left her hometown, her life, her friends, her family and her dreams all just to make a difference.

THE REAL STORY

MONDAY, SEPTEMBER 26ᵀᴴ
FENTON, MICHIGAN
8:50 A.M.

The morning was chilled, and droopy raindrops splashed onto my windshield. I flipped my wipers on trying to peer through the haziness. I was down-shifting into third gear when my cell phone rang. I was in the process of turning, as I expertly downshifted to second, maneuvered the steering wheel to the right and slid my phone open.

"Hello," I answered as I shifted again.

"Rose, it's Jan from the Red Cross." She didn't wait for me to respond. "We've received your deployment orders. You need to be at Headquarters at noon today to receive your paperwork and deployment briefing. We will need you to catch the earliest flight out."

I paused, shifting into fourth gear. My thoughts were racing. *Whoa! Ok, sure, let me just go hop on a plane, and hope that magically my bills will be paid on time and my car will somehow still be there when I return. Pack? Who needs time to pack? Work? Who needs a two-week notice? C'mon let's be serious!*

In the midst of my confusion, I heard myself respond, "Sure, I'll be there at noon."

As I slid my phone shut, I inwardly prayed that there would be no available flights that day somehow. I needed at least 24 hours to prepare. *I couldn't believe they were deploying me already!* I had just finished my training the day before. It wasn't supposed to be this soon! I wondered if any of the other participants in my training class had been called too or if I was the only one. *Well I guess I would find out!*

THE RED CROSS
HOWELL, MICHIGAN
12:00 P.M.

I glanced at the sole, bright red cross, stark against the white background, marking the only sign that designated the building behind it, as a Red Cross building.

The parking lot was already swamped with puddles as I slipped my Mustang into a spot near the front. I grabbed my notepad and pen, pulled my jacket tight around me as I locked my car and entered the building.

A deep sense of trepidation filled me then. Not one of fear but one of curiosity. Where was this journey going to take me? I had never embarked on an adventure such as this before, and minute-by-minute the future was unraveling right before my eyes. It was such a quixotic moment.

The next several hours slipped by in slow motion as I was briefed on my destination city, Baton Rouge. I processed through paperwork, and listened to information on what to expect on the Operation.

Later that evening, I sent an email to all my contacts concerning my deployment and explaining my quick disappearance.

MONDAY, SEPTEMBER 26th
EMAIL COORESPONDENCE
7:30 P.M.

Dear All,

I know I have to be one of the hardest people to keep up with and even harder to keep track of. <smile> I'm not very good at sending little notices of "Where in the World is Rose?", for my travels around the world take me far away from all of you too often to pen on paper at times.

I only have a few brief moments to send this quick email of my latest escapade.

I recently enlisted and trained with the Red Cross to aid in the recent hurricane disaster relief operation. I got a call early this morning to catch the earliest possible flight out to Baton Rouge, Louisiana. I am glad to say that all available flights are booked until Thursday, September 29th, which still allows me two days to prepare for my absence rather than just a few hours.

At this point, I am scheduled to return from a three-week assignment on October 20th. I will not find out until I arrive in Baton Rouge of my assignment position or the location I will be sent to from there. I have been told that I may stay in Louisiana, or be sent to Texas.

I received a debit card today from the Red Cross for expenses so I'm going shopping tomorrow. (JUST KIDDING!). The card is strictly for food and supplies and is pre-loaded with $1,000, to last me for a month.

Because I don't know any more information...I can't give you any more details. However, I do know that I won't have computer access and that most landlines are out of service. I am authorized to use a cell phone but not guaranteed coverage with all of the damaged towers.

I was told that I am to take a small blanket, a flashlight, summer clothes and some other handy necessities. I will be sleeping on the floor or on a cot if I am lucky. It kind of bugs me that some of the other volunteers were complaining about the sleeping conditions and about not being able to sleep on mattresses.

Honestly, what do they expect? Is it just me or did a hurricane just come through and take away everything those people owned? I would give them the shirt off my back before wasting my time complaining about not having decent enough accommodations! Seriously!

Anyways...I've been told I'll be working a minimum of 12-hour shifts daily. Taking pictures will be difficult, but I'm sure I'll be able to swing a *couple of photos. <smile> Well, I'm going to get some sleep.*

Somewhere out there,

Rosie the Riveter

THURSDAY, SEPTEMBER 29th
DEPARTURE MORNING
8:00 A.M.

The rapid beeping of my alarm roused me from a dreamy sleep. I slowly opened my eyes as I pulled the soft covers tighter around me. There was a bitter chill wafting through the air and my skin was frozen like a block of ice. This was typical Michigan weather. It would be eighty degrees one minute and ten minutes later, cold enough to wear a winter coat! It is very temperamental here, and this morning a gentle frost had iced the tips of the grass blades.

Today was the big day. It felt almost surreal. The only thing I knew was what time my flight was leaving and the destination to which it was going. I wouldn't know where I would sleep, stay, work, eat, shower, or anything else until my plane landed.

I basically wouldn't find out any more details of my deployment till after I arrived in Baton Rouge at 10:00 p.m. It was kind of exciting. Hmmm...and deliciously adventurous! What's more, it's hard to be prepared for something you know so little about. I guess it made it that much more intriguing.

I'm a planner. I like to know the details of life's events so I can always be successful. But here I didn't have that, and in a way, it was a test for me. Because of the circumstances, I would have to be confident and prepared to handle anything that came my way. I was all by myself here, and I didn't have any supervisor or boss to offer helpful guidance. I was all alone.

I finally crawled out from underneath my cocoon of warmth and padded into the bathroom. The tiled floor was cool to my feet, and goosebumps flared up on my arms. I turned to close the door behind me when all of the sudden something caused me to pause in my tracks. Something felt funny deep inside my chest and my breathing picked up rapidly as I tried to quell this awful feeling.

Suddenly, a powerful surge of choking attacked my lungs. I grabbed my chest and ran over to the sink as I coughed violently into the small recess. I was coughing so roughly that tears began to fall down my cheeks, and my breath was coming out in ragged gasps.

My eyes froze in that instant when I noticed thin spatters of deep red blood spotting the sink. I didn't have time to think as another racking cough assailed me. This time, there was so much blood I just stared at it not believing it was there. *Oh no! What was happening!*

I just stood there with my hand over my mouth trying to will away the horror of what I was seeing. *How could this be?* The doctor had given me a very strong antibiotic over 10 days prior. The strep-pneumonia should be gone, not getting worse. I knew the cold weather was the culprit and it was making my cough hang on.

I quickly turned the faucet on to destroy any evidence of the incident. With my heart racing, I went back into the bedroom falling weakly back on the bed. My hands were shaking as I closed my eyes and swallowed thickly.

I pulled the blanket over my chilled body as I considered my options. First, I wasn't going to tell anyone of the incident. They would just worry. Second, I couldn't tell the Red Cross that I was sick. I had just promised them that I would go down South to help people way worse off than me. They would think of me as careless. Besides, I had already booked my flight and packed my bags. It just didn't seem right. Plus, it was just a cough, and I'm sure with the warm air down South I would be just fine.

After much pondering, I came to the conclusion that I just didn't have time to be sick. I would just pretend that nothing had happened this morning and hope that I didn't get worse. The chill of the morning was the only plausible reason for this outlandish relapse. *Sometimes I hated Michigan weather!* I would just have to tough it out.

I had just gotten back to finishing my packing and had put the incident into the back of my mind when another bout assailed me. I ran into the bathroom again as several more racking coughs shook my body. This time my shock turned into frustrated anger. I felt as if some unseen force was trying to prevent me from getting on that plane. I felt as if something was goading me, maliciously taunting me. It didn't seem fair.

I felt like I was finally trying to do something good and meaningful in my life, and it was all just going to unravel right in front of me. I willed my mind to focus on leaving Michigan and began to pray that some miracle would befall me and heal my cough in time for my arrival in Baton Rouge.

THURSDAY, SEPTEMBER 29th
TOUCHDOWN: BATON ROUGE
10:30 P.M.

I grabbed my two matching blue duffel bags and exited the plane. A great sense of excitement filled me then. Disembarking the plane was the final piece of information that I was aware of on this trip.

I was already a world traveler. I spent most of my savings and hard earned pennies traveling the world since I was sixteen years old. I was fascinated with other cultures and enjoyed studying many foreign languages and speaking them around the world. I was used to well-planned trips and formulated itineraries. This was a whole new ballgame for me that I wasn't used to.

Where would I sleep tonight? Would the Red Cross Headquarters here be closed? Was I the only person here at this time of night arriving from the Red Cross? Would I even get sleep tonight or would I have to process paperwork at Headquarters till the early hours of the morning?

The incident with my lingering cough was shoved into the back of my mind as the adrenaline force of my mission took over. I had been told that when I arrived in Baton Rouge I was supposed to call a special number to find out my next set of orders. It was like a treasure hunt almost, where one clue led to the next, except this wasn't a hunt but a journey. *It is already so late, would anyone answer the phone?*

I walked into the terminal and headed over to a deserted gate to set my bags down on a group of empty seats. I rubbed my sore shoulders for a brief moment after the weight of my luggage had been taken off. I reached into my jean's right pocket and pulled out a small piece of paper that had a special telephone number on it, slid my cell phone open and punched it in.

I admit, having already become an avid traveler despite my youth did nothing to take away the strange feeling I had on this particular late night. I wasn't flying here to visit someone, for vacation, or for business. I had never done something like this before. Even flying to Costa Rica and living there for a time in the mountains, where no one spoke English, didn't compare to this eerie feeling.

In a sense, it was an amazing thought. I was finally about to do something in my life for someone else. I had literally dropped everything to fly into the madness of Hurricane Katrina to help the victims. I had flown in to help people I didn't even know and individuals that I would probably never even see again. It was courageous and commendable.

Never had I felt such a feeling before. I can't explain it. It was just so wonderful to stand there, not even knowing what to do next or what lay ahead but to know it would all be worth it. I decided to make a vow that no matter what was to happen in the next three weeks, I would give all of my time, talent and skills to make a difference.

Yes, I wanted to help make food, find housing for the homeless or find clothes and supplies for them, but I also wanted to make sure I didn't leave until I saw the tears and hopelessness on their faces turn into smiles of happiness again. I wanted to give them hope for a whole new beginning, that they could begin to believe in again.

There were very few people in the terminal and there was a large silence filling the emptiness during the late hour. A deep weariness had already begun to fill my body. I felt sluggish from the long day of traveling and already sleepy from the late hour.

The phone rang several times before an automated reply came on. I was surprised to get a recorded message and frowned for a moment wondering if they were closed and if I would have to sleep at the airport.

A woman's voice came on and explained that it was after hours, Headquarters was closed and all Disaster Relief (DR) 865 members arriving on evening flights, were to wait for the next available shuttle to be taken to a nearby shelter, to sleep for the night.

In the morning, transportation would be provided to take all incoming Disaster Relief 865 members to Headquarters to receive assignments. The number 865 identified my group, the latest group of volunteers arriving in Baton Rouge from the Red Cross. I hung up the phone and picked up my duffels.

I was adjusting my Red Cross ID Badge when I noticed a man old enough to be my father, standing nearby at a pay phone booth. He was wearing a large white t-shirt with a large red cross on the back. On a whim I approached him, and asked if he was an 865 member. He was!

He kindly introduced himself as John and I smiled and told him my name was Rose. He said that he hadn't been able to get through to the recording on the pay phone so I quickly told him what it had said. He expressed sincere thanks for my assistance and proceeded to follow me to the airport entrance to pick up our shuttle.

Unbeknownst to me, the adventures had not even begun yet. It would be mere hours from now that a gunshot would change everything.

THURSDAY, SEPTEMBER 29th
HOWELL PARK
THE SHOOTING
11:20 P.M.

Inside the shuttle alongside a small group of other incoming stragglers, I peered out the window as we slowly drove down unfamiliar, empty streets. There were a few lights here and there from the roadside posts, but not a lot of activity going on. There were very few cars on the road and it seemed strange to see it so calm, even having never been to Baton Rouge before.

I was trying my best to follow my orders and didn't want to ask any questions. I had no idea where we were going and kept looking out the window, not making conversation with anyone else in the bus. I knew we were being taken somewhere to sleep for the night and nothing else.

I felt alone and out of place stuck on a bus with random people from all over the United States. It was awkward and clear to see that everyone was way older than me, most by twenty years. I started to get the feeling that I would be one of the youngest people to have come here and didn't know if that was a good or a bad thing. We had nothing in common except for the very reason we had come to Baton Rouge; to help.

I decided just to remain strong and tough it out until the morning when I knew where I would be sent to work. At least when I got my job assignment, I could start to feel of some use.

We pulled into a gloomy looking park. Unbeknownst to us this was in a very dangerous section of Baton Rouge, a place where criminal activity was common place. In reality, we would find that any place in Louisiana could be dangerous at this time because of the devastated state it was in. However, tonight would give us our first big realization of that.

The Park's Recreation Building had been turned into a temporary Staff Shelter we soon found out.

We waited in the van to find out if the shelter had room for us. Luckily they did. We wearily unloaded out of the vehicle and began to sift through the luggage to find our personal bags. By the time I had gathered all my belongings, everyone had already gone inside the facility. I turned around and headed up the sidewalk towards the entrance.

It was a moonlit night filled with millions of glittering stars. The air was warm and a welcome relief to my sore throat. I walked purposely and eagerly up to the entrance; I didn't know what to expect and was only thinking of finally laying my head down to sleep.

The front door reminded me of a large barn door. It was huge, heavy, and rolled on wheels that pushed to the right and was large enough to fit a car through. I pulled the heavy door open, curious to see what lie on the other side. I stepped inside and just stood there. I did a double-take, blinking my eyes to make sure that what I was seeing was real. I didn't know if I was ready for this.

Walking around the corner and peering in the doorway, my heart seemed to forget to beat for a second. There were over a hundred cots strewn all over an empty, wooden, brown floor, every single one of them filled with volunteers. The harsh lights of the high ceiling seemed to glare ominously at me and I almost took a step backward. I swallowed thickly as I noticed all of the saddened eyes now turned on me.

Suddenly the large door slammed shut behind me, causing me to jump at the loud, jarring crash. I felt chagrined almost, as my gaze swept over the room taking in every single person clinging to their blankets, the one thing that they knew belonged to them here. It was their sole comfort and the one connection that reminded them of the place that they had come from. It was a stark realization of what I had gotten myself into by flying into Baton Rouge, leaving my safe haven back in Michigan. It all started to sink in during those brief moments as I just stood there. I was starting to have second thoughts.

I've always had really nice things in my life. Growing up at home before I had gotten my first apartment, my father had worked very hard to make sure that my other siblings and I were well provided for and had need of nothing. I had lived in a really large, beautiful home with a wrap-around porch, plenty of property with riding trails and hunting grounds, a swimming pond with a beach and a windmill, an indoor floor hockey rink and basketball court, pool table, ping pong table, piano, popcorn machine, workout room, nice cars, you name it.

My mother had been a stay at home mom that always made the most amazing home-cooked meals and desserts, did our laundry and helped in any way she could. All seven of us kids were able to have our own bedrooms and design them ourselves. I knew what it was like to have nice things and had never had anything different.

My breath caught in my throat and warm, wet tears welled up in my eyes. I didn't know how to react to this. I gripped the large door handle for support as I just stood there. It was a breath-catching moment that totally immobilized me for a second. What I saw was shocking and I felt out of place and scared in that moment.

The hurricane coverage that I saw on TV was sad, shocking and moving, but there was nothing that could have prepared me for what I saw in person. Nothing! It is easy to see the footage on TV and then go on with your life because you are disassociated by location. You know that your life isn't affected and it's easy to ignore it in a sense. I came from a very privileged life and I just wasn't prepared for the quick change that began to take place on this very night.

I said a silent prayer of thanks as someone to my right led me over to a small table to sign in. I found out that there were no cots left for me. I wasn't surprised.

All I had brought with me to sleep with was a small, purple blanket with Tinkerbell on it. I hadn't brought a pillow so I wouldn't have the extra weight to carry. I am a pretty adaptable girl when it comes down to it, and I had been forewarned that sleeping conditions would be arduous, so I tried to bear with the changes as best I could.

The building was packed and I already felt like an intruder. I didn't need a cot, and I didn't want to impose anymore, especially anyone who was trying to fall asleep. I felt like I just needed a moment alone and since I was the last person to come in for the night, I knew everyone was waiting for the lights to be shut off.

It was a beautiful night outside and the peace and solitude beckoned me. I turned to the Shelter Manager and asked permission to sleep outside in the grass considering the circumstances, even offering her a small smile to let her know that I truly didn't mind. She calmly said she didn't think that it would be safe for me to sleep outside alone and that I should just find a sleeping place in the corner for tonight.

I wouldn't know until several hours later that her answer saved my life. I smiled a brief note of acceptance and turned around to step through the maze of cots to the opposite end of the facility where two large doors had been propped open to let the fresh air circulate the building. I noticed an empty spot just inside the doorway and set down my bags; it was the only available space left and the furthest away from everyone else.

I pulled out my blanket, laid it out on the wooden floor and stuffed a pile of clothes at one end for a pillow. I collapsed on the blanket in exhaustion, too spent to change clothes. I laid out on the hard surface, letting the warm air from the outside rush over me like a comforting blanket. I closed my eyes deeply drinking in the Southern air trying to calm the racing thoughts in my mind. I admit it was rather lonesome.

I felt completely displaced from the comfort of home and familiarity. I was lying in a room full of people, yet people that I didn't know at all and still hundreds of miles from home…and this was just the beginning.

I still had three weeks left, three weeks of unknown circumstances, living out of two duffel bags with not even a promise of a bed, shower, or toilet. I had tried to prepare myself for this, but I realized that it wasn't going to be anything I had expected.

I felt even more out of place because I was one of the youngest people in the building. Quickly looking around, I realized I was probably the only twenty-one-year-old there! Everyone was older; if anything, most were probably retired from the looks of it!

This was real. The reality of the rapid change in my life was hitting me then and I almost wished I hadn't come. I berated myself for my negative thought and reminded myself that this wasn't about me. If I was going to be of any help down here, I was going to have to be strong.

I shoved the uneasy feelings into the back of my mind and concentrated on falling asleep. The lights turned off just then with a loud pop, and a deep silence closed over the room. The only sounds heard were soft snores and sporadic coughing. I peeked out at the stars realizing in that moment that someone far away was looking up at those same stars, and that sometimes, the stars might be the only thing that connects you to that special someone you love.

I don't know how much time had passed at this point. I wondered if I was the only person that was still awake. My mind was still going a million miles an hour and despite my exhaustion, I couldn't shut out all the snores and coughs around me to disappear into oblivion.

My mind started to drift to another time, and another place as it often does when my imagination takes over. I was thinking of the time I was in Germany when I had shockingly eaten an entire basket of sweet-rolls in one sitting, and had been too embarrassed to put on a bathing suit later on that eve to go swimming.

I had been scared that everyone would see the rolls sitting in my stomach! I had eaten at least twelve of them! I was reminiscing about these memories when a loud thud caused my back to stiffen. I waited a few moments, wondering if I was just hearing things. I was all alone near this doorway and everyone else was still sleeping further inside the building. I'm not one to get scared easily, but my intuition told me that something was not right.

My exhaustion was quickly forgotten as I scooted away from the open doorway to the edge of the door to hide. I froze as I heard angry voices, picking up in intensity to my right. I didn't dare poke my head out until I knew more of what was going on. My heart was racing. *What should I do?*

I sat with my back on the edge of the wall next to the door. I knew they couldn't see me; even more, I assumed that they didn't know there was a room full of people in here. I didn't have time to think anymore. The piercing pop of a gunshot split the thick night air.

Oh my God! I clamped my lips together to hold in a silent scream. I couldn't move. I couldn't do anything. My eyes were opened wide and my entire body was frozen in place. *Someone just got shot!*

I realized then, that I couldn't do anything. To show myself, would be to show the entire room of sleeping people. It would put everyone at risk and several people were already beginning to stir. I didn't have time to think any longer. A sudden swarm of police cars with lights flashing, and sirens blazing, zoomed around the corner to the scene.

By now, several people inside the shelter were awake and were heading over to the doorway where I hid. Hiding behind the cloak of darkness, I slid back onto my blanket and pretended to be asleep. The police had already taken over, and I was feeling a little too traumatized to risk moving for the moment. I concentrated on "sleeping" while the Shelter Manager and co-manager assessed the situation outside.

The next several hours passed by in a blur. The police arrested the murderer and an ambulance took away the victim…albeit he was already dead. The Shelter Manager quickly popped back inside the shelter, pulling both double doors closed and locking them. Shockingly, most everyone was still asleep and it would be morning before they had a clue that a crime had even happened.

I sniffed softly as tears pooled in my eyes. It was pitch black now that all the doors were closed, and my tears fell silently, hidden thereupon. They were tears of sadness and pain, tears of udder befuddlement at the cruelty of mankind and the audacity in which one man could have such hatred to take the life of another human being. It was so wrong. My lips were pressed together in anger and I tried to breathe deeply to calm the pounding in my chest. After hearing the gunshot outside, it was as if some unseen force enveloped me and gave me a renewed sense of strength. *This is why I am here,* I thought. I came here to make a difference and this is my place right now. There are good people here, and we are going to help them. We have to.

I don't remember sleeping that night. I just kept tossing and turning on the hard floor trying to shut out the memories of what had just happened.

It wasn't long before 6:00 a.m. rolled around, and the lights in the shelter were flipped on to wake everyone. It was time to get up and pack our belongings to drive over to Headquarters.

I wrapped up my little Tinkerbell blanket and pulled out a fresh change of clothes. I left my luggage in a pile and headed towards the front door. I noticed another building close by and assumed that was where the bathrooms were. I am not a morning person, so I felt too grumpy to just simply ask someone where they were at.

I headed over that way and walked up the steps to the adjoining building. I followed the cardboard sign that had a black arrow colored in with magic marker that pointed to the left saying "Women".

I entered in through a wooden plank door that was hanging ajar on rusty hinges. My steps slowed as I walked inside. A rank musty odor seared my nostrils and a prickly chill crept over my bones. Several weak light bulbs hung precariously from the ceiling casting shadows across the large room. Cobwebs hung eerily from the corners and the drip, drip, drip of a running faucet pinched the silence.

My head whipped to the right as I heard a squeaky faucet slowly turning. I turned my head away abashed when I noticed the naked backside of a young woman standing in the dark alcove that stood for a shower. It just seemed eerie that this whole dilapidated bathroom was deemed usable.

I grimaced as angry images of the Holocaust gas chambers flitted through my mind. It was such a creepy place to be called a bathroom with makeshift showers and absolutely no doors or walls for privacy, I couldn't think of anything to compare it to except to the terrifying concentration camps of World War II.

I quickened my pace and headed over to where two elderly toilets lay in the back corner. There were no doors. If you wanted privacy, you'd best go outside in the bushes. I shyly pulled down my pants and went to the bathroom, trying to ignore the other random women coming in and out of the hideous room.

There is no way I was taking a shower here. I admit I just wasn't ready to strip naked on this early morning in front of peering eyes and mischievous spiders. I would wait and pray that tonight I would be stationed somewhere else that offered better hygiene conditions. I'm a skinny little thing, nothing to be ashamed of, but still uncomfortable here, and definitely not in the mood.

FRIDAY, SEPTEMBER 30th
RED CROSS HEADQUARTERS
BATON ROUGE, LOUISIANA
7:00 A.M.

We arrived in convoys at an abandoned Wal-mart that had been turned into the main Headquarters for the Hurricane Katrina Relief Operation in Louisiana. It was about 20 minutes away from Howell Park. We gathered our belongings and headed up to the front gate to show our badges to gain entrance to the facility.

After being cleared, we were told to drop our luggage within the gated-off entranceway and then head inside the building. I was hesitant to leave my luggage outside, because anyone could just walk away with it. Nonetheless, those were my orders and I followed them.

I headed inside the double doors and paused for a moment to take it all in. The first thing I noticed was a craze of huge posters that had been made into signs and were hung everywhere. It reminded me of a military operation.

Every department was labeled with titles such as Homeland Security, Feeding, Sheltering, Health Services, Client Services, Networking, RTT, Public Relations and more. A little room off to the left had a little sign above the doorway that said, "Oasis", which was a little beverage/snack center for the volunteers.

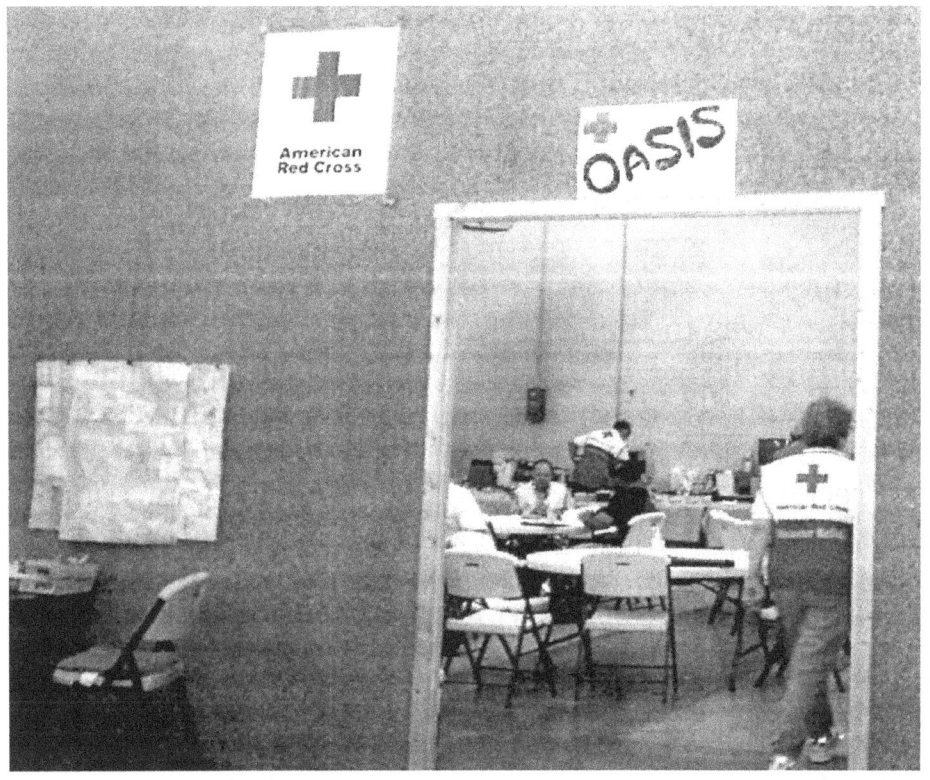

The oasis in the middle of crisis! It was a very charming surprise. This building was the main Headquarters in Louisiana that had been created to facilitate all of the Red Cross relief efforts throughout the entire state. As organized as it seemed, with all of the signs posted, I got the feeling that it was more of a madhouse right now than a calm, professional post.

Since I had landed in Baton Rouge, nothing had struck me as normal here. Nothing was. As each minute passed, I would learn that everything that happened during my time down here would teach me what it was like to be in the middle of a true disaster-stricken world.

ORIENTATION
8:00 A.M.

After handing in our identification papers, we were sent in groups of 40 to the back corner of the building for our Operation Katrina Orientation. Lucky for me, I was in the first group of the day, so I didn't have to wait.

A somewhat comical man got up in front of a huge white board to greet us all. As he began to speak, we all received a thick packet telling us of the "Do's and Don'ts" of the operation. It also detailed the facts and statistics of Katrina and all its counterparts following the relief efforts. We learned the immediate basics of Louisiana itself, including the fact that it contained many hazards that Michigan could never compete with.

Louisiana is home to the poisonous brown recluse spider, fierce fire ants that bite harder than you can imagine, and many large alligators that were now homeless and forced to relocate into the streets and cities after the hurricane.

Even more exciting to find out was the fact that the United States is home to four poisonous snakes. Lucky for us, Louisiana contained all four snakes. (I'm being sarcastic on the "lucky" part!)

Worse, we were told that dysentery was rampant here and because of it, we were ordered to use hand sanitizer every 10 minutes if possible. As I looked around, I noticed that there were hand sanitizer bottles lying on every table and counter top. It left a creepy feeling in my mind to know that it only took touching one wrong thing and this trip could be over. Going to the bathroom after that made me want to plug my nose so I wouldn't breathe in any germs, and even more, I was scared to touch anything. The threat of such disease and health risks was kind of nerve-wracking!

Our orientation guy left us with one last pressing reminder: to drink water, and plenty of it. We were told we would not last on our trip down here if we did not drink non-stop. The intense Southern heat would dehydrate our bodies so quickly, and the threat of contamination would make us sicker much faster than dysentery would.

I kind of laughed inwardly at the guide's intense almost comical remarks when he was stressing the water factor. I personally hated to drink much of anything. On a normal basis, I was lucky if I would drink a glass of water in a day! I was like, *"Yeah, drink water? That would be a miracle in itself!"*

It wouldn't be until I started throwing up later on that day, that I would shove the sarcasm down my throat, and realize, that if I didn't want to be sent home, I would have to heed our guide's words. He wasn't kidding around. The conditions down here were arduous and hard. And when the conditions change, so do your circumstances. If you don't learn to adapt fast and immediately, you won't be in any condition to help anyone else.

ASSIGNMENT ORDERS
9:00 A.M.

I stood in line to go through the paperwork process and pick up my specific assignment. I didn't know what to expect and was really curious to see what the Red Cross had chosen for me. They took each volunteer's skills, talents, current and past job history to place them in a department where they would be used the most.

The assignments ranged from feeding the victims in the client shelters, to finding homes for the victims, to assisting the victims medically, to making sure the security of all these efforts was in place and all of the volunteers and clients were protected. They used the word "client" for the evacuees.

I wasn't picky about which assignment I would be given. My only hope was that whatever work orders I received, I would be good at my job and try to help as many people as one person could possibly help in the three weeks I would be here.

Never could I have been more surprised to be assigned to Safety and Security. This department was the smallest, and currently had only 30 people working in it, out of the average 22,000 others, who were volunteering in Louisiana at this time.

Safety and Security's job was: to make sure that all of the volunteers were safe, that the victims being helped were safe, that all criminal occurrences would be documented and reported to the police, that guards were placed at all the shelters and on duty twenty-four hours a day, that the Red Cross was set up and working in every hurricane stricken part of Louisiana, and that the operation would be kept secure and ongoing no matter what crises affected the relief efforts.

I was the only female in the group other than the secretary of the department. The rest were EMTs, fireman, police officers, military persons or those of criminal law-enforcement backgrounds. My background was a little different, but as I would find out, that difference was just what this department needed.

I own a private Foreign Language Company in Michigan in which I translate, interpret, and instruct in six languages for clients in the United States and Internationally. I have a degree in Foreign Language and professional interpreting experience.

I also work as the Deputy Registrar for the local government office, running all public elections; including the Presidential Elections to Special School Elections.

I have a lot of experience working with the public, including interpreting for professional sports athletes, assisting patients in the hospitals that don't speak English, interpreting in the Courts for the arraignments of criminals, and more. I have also volunteered my entire life for a non-profit organization called "Send the Light". This Outreach was started by my family to help the less-fortunate around the world.

I am great at multi-tasking and running my own company at such a young age. I can also shoot a gun and am skilled at hand-to-hand combat. I am an innovative thinker and passionate about implementing new ideas that make even a good situation better. Despite my accomplishments in my line of work, I was mainly selected for Safety and Security for my people skills and experience in dealing with public issues.

Down here, there was a lot of confusion amongst incoming volunteers and a clear lack of order on the Operation with the constant changeover of workers. Volunteers came to help for three weeks and then were sent back home once the new replacements flew in. Any system that was set up previously, was hard to keep going once the positions were replaced with new people coming in. This caused constant tension and disarray.

I could already feel the pressure and stress as I observed the crowds of people around me. I could see people literally running from department to department as if the world was going to end. It wasn't a calm place…no, it was complete chaos and utter madness. As I stood there, I wondered if anyone was really in charge. It seemed as if no one knew what to do, where to go, or how to connect and meet in the middle.

There were several hundred people packed in this huge room right now, with mere posters on the walls labeling each department section. I raised an eyebrow as I wondered if this was the situation every day.

I glanced up just then as a man came running into the building with his fists barred, charging through as if he was drunk. He was shouting something along the lines that a tornado had just touched down and was coming towards us.

I moved around a group of people to reaffirm that the sunlight outside was still there and stood stock still as I watched him barrel past. I wanted to roll my eyes at the crazy man, but at the same time I understood that a lot of people weren't used to dealing with a crisis of this magnitude; it quickly brought out the weakest part of those that couldn't handle the pressure. I would find out later that those people were sent back home early.

One of the first things my new boss would tell me ended up being a sort of comfort I clung to for the rest of the operation. "It's hard for people to argue with a calm, young, beautiful girl like you. We need someone with your charm and personality to keep people from going at each other's throats. You have such a bright smile and it's rare to see any smiles here. I think you're going to be great for us." And when I heard that, I realized that being young perhaps was not a bad thing anymore here. Perhaps he would be right.

And that was that. I was stationed at Headquarters in Baton Rouge. About 95% of the people that arrived at Headquarters to pick up job assignments were immediately re-sent out to a field station at a separate location in Louisiana. I happened to be one of the few people that would be stationed to work directly at Headquarters right here in this building. I found out later that was a good thing. Here I would have Internet access and cell phone service so I'd be able to communicate with the people back home.

In addition, there was a Health Services Department for immediate medical attention almost right next to Safety and Security (SAS) should I get sick. It was comforting to know that help was close in case any disease or contamination threats should interfere with my stay here.

I finished my paperwork up at the SAS department and was promised a rental car and a motel room for the duration of my deployment! I couldn't believe it. I would actually have a real shower later that night! *How lucky was I!* I felt so dirty at this point, and even more than that, completely weary. It had now been almost 48 hours since I'd slept or eaten.

It was about this moment in the middle of the madness that I started to feel faint. My stomach began to tighten and cramp in anger at the fallibility of me to feed it properly and my mouth suddenly went dry. I tried to concentrate on the words my SAS boss was telling me, but all of the sudden his words drifted off. I felt a strange flush rush over my body and I knew I going to be sick. I somehow stammered that I had to go, and tried to valiantly disguise a calm run to the bathroom.

It was quite some way to the bathroom, considering the fact that it was holed up in the back of the building. I don't even know how I made it in time. I rushed into one of the empty stalls and vomited roughly into the toilet. Since I hadn't eaten or drank anything since arriving here, the persistent heaves were very painful. My body was mad and I would suffer for it. I calmly flushed the toilet, washed my hands, and returned to SAS pretending as if nothing had happened.

I had a job here to do…that's all that mattered. I grabbed some snacks and drinks from the "Oasis" and quickly munched on those.

THE BOMB THREAT
10:35 A.M.

I didn't have time to think about being sick anymore, because as soon as I returned to my department, my boss (a Lieutenant Colonel in the Army) gave me my first assignment.

"I need you to go outside and figure out why we have a ticking suitcase in the luggage area," he said calmly.

For my first assignment, I didn't expect a potential bomb threat to be something of my expertise. I felt my heart skip a beat at the possibility of a terrorist infiltration and had no more time to think as a fellow police officer grabbed my arm and pulled me towards the door.

It would be almost too easy for a terrorist to walk right into the madness and lay down a single blow that would fatally cripple the entire operation. This fear would never leave my mind, nor would it ever dissipate due to the very real possibility that it could happen.

I hurriedly walked next to the police officer as we rushed outside to where two security guards stood over a stack of two green duffel bags and a black backpack. My heart started to beat faster as the strong tick-tock of a steady beat ominously protruded from the luggage pile. Everyone was just standing there frozen, and unsure of what to do.

The guards had reported the incident and were waiting on us to fix it. Nobody wanted to touch anything, and our group from Safety and Security didn't want to go searching through people's luggage without authorization. Then again, we also didn't want to exclude the possibility that someone could have planted a bomb within the security fence putting the lives of several hundred people at risk. Keeping in mind, these were also the people that were spearheading the Red Cross Katrina Relief Operation, facilitating and networking the relief efforts throughout the entire state of Louisiana. We couldn't take that risk.

Nobody was moving, and nobody was saying anything. I was baffled. I'm not one to wait around for something bad to happen. I figure if I have to wait around all the time for someone else to do it first…it may never happen. I just couldn't understand why I was the only one that wasn't scared either, with professional police officers sitting right beside me.

So while everyone was standing there frozen in contemplation, I began to move. Everyone stepped a few feet back just staring as I crouched down and tried to pinpoint which bag the ticking was coming from. I pulled the first bag off the pile and pressed my left ear against the second one instantly realized that the ticking was coming from that bag.

I figured if it really was a bomb, most bombs were timed in some way. So the faster that we moved, the more time we would have to stop the bomb. Also though, some bombs were set to go off if they were touched or an attached sensor was pulled before you could even locate the bomb. There were several important possibilities for sure, but the constant "tick-tocking" reminded me that we still had time. *How much though?*

Everyone in our little group stepped back even further as I pulled the black backpack off the pile and gently placed in the middle of the cement floor.

Nobody reached down to help. Nobody wanted to touch it! I didn't even care at this point. I wasn't going to wait for a bomb to blow up in my face if that was the case. My heart pounded in anticipation for what I would find; I prayed that it would be nothing similar to what everyone feared. I leaned in close to the dark bag again trying to pinpoint which zipper the sound was coming from.

Since I'd lost half my hearing in my right ear earlier in my lifetime, I was having difficulty at this point. I took a guess and slowly pulled open the main zipper of the backpack. My eyes widened as I noticed a clear Ziploc bag full of dark orange medication bottles. There had to have been 10 or 15 large bottles of drugs. I gingerly reached in and pulled the Ziploc bag back peering underneath. At this point, all I saw was a stash of bunched up clothes and a few pairs of socks. I realized then that the ticking was coming from the outside pocket.

I quickly re-zipped the large zipper and glanced up at my comrades who were just watching me with serious stares. I blew at a wisp of hair in my face in exasperation. Little did I know that this wouldn't be the last time on the operation that I would be the only one willing to make a move...in fact, it would be the first of many.

I pressed my lips firmly together as I went back to turning the backpack on it's back. I was getting antsy at this point. It seemed like it was taking forever to pinpoint the "tick-tocking" sound and "forever" wasn't an option in situations like this. I hurriedly (yet carefully) tore open the outer pocket and abruptly stepped back as our tick-tock culprit was exposed.

I fell backwards, spent from the whole ordeal, and sat on the ground taking in the sight before me. I wiped a drop of sweat off my brow and glanced at the others. I felt my heart rate return to normal and I heard the guards and the officer beside me breathe a sigh of relief at the sight of a small, brown alarm clock staring back at them from the opened pocket of the backpack.

The officer that had accompanied me from SAS let out a little laugh as he reached down and shut the alarm off. He wasn't laughing because it was funny, but rather laughing in relief! The tension that bound us moments before dissipated in that instant.

"Good job, Rose," the officer said as he reached over to pat me lightly on the shoulder.

I flashed him a quick smile. I got up slowly and followed him back to Safety and Security while the guards went back to their duties.

SAFETY AND SECURITY DEPARTMENT
9:16 P.M.

The rest of the day found me writing up incident reports. Incident reports were similar to police reports and detailed the date, time, and place of criminal occurrences and offenses on the operation. I was thankful to at least be sitting down while I was working. My body was still very weak with exhaustion from lack of sleep, vomiting, and not being able to eat any real food since I'd arrived here.

It was after 9:00 p.m. when through blurry eyes I saw someone hand me the keys to a rental vehicle and a little scrap of paper that had a nearby motel address. My eyes peeked open a little wider at the thought of having actual motel accommodations for my post of duty in Baton Rouge. There was a glimmer of hope inside of me that I would be able to get my body's health back up to par and gain strength to continue working at my best.

I would be one of the few people that would be able to return home with the story of having a vehicle and a motel on the operation. I not only felt lucky, but I also felt that God had sent a little miracle my way, just when I needed it the most.

About 95% of the 22,000 or so Red Cross volunteers on the current operation were staying in staff shelters. A staff shelter was a church, gym, or vacant building that had been turned into a makeshift housing arrangement for the volunteers to sleep in after their duties. Some shelters had the showers outside in makeshift tents called haz-mats, where others had one-room showers as previously mentioned with Howell Park. Every shelter's sleeping quarters consisted of one large room filled with cots. There was no privacy, no quietness, and nowhere to relax, be alone or even protect your belongings. I would later find out, that even in a motel room your belongings weren't safe.

    I breathed a huge sigh of relief as the enticing thoughts of a hot shower, clean towels and a warm bed filled my imagination. I felt like the luckiest girl alive, especially after what had happened the previous night at Howell Park. It was a miracle, and unbeknownst to me, it would be the first of many to come on the operation.

    I gathered my duffels and simple belongings and headed out into the black night. The warm, Southern air again hit me like a soft pillow, enveloping me with a hug of warmth. I loved it. There was just something about fresh air and the still of a black night that made me feel comforted.

    I glanced up at the stars again, the one calm, constant factor that captivated the evening sky. I called out a quiet "goodnight" to the guards standing at the fenced in entrance to the building I had just left, and headed out towards the parking lot. I had been told that my vehicle was in the row of cars just outside the Red Cross barricade. The barricade itself was simply cordoning off a large section of the parking lot for all of the vehicles used by Headquarters.

    Because of the late hour, the parking lot was empty and devoid of any activity. There were rows and rows of cars and as my droopy eyes scanned over them, I didn't even think that a lone girl walking around a large parking lot in the black of night wasn't a very safe idea. I had never seen the car before and had no clue what it looked like or what color it was. I felt stupid, for the only thing I knew was that it was a vehicle of some sort!

There were so many cars, trucks, and SUVs; in my weariness the shapes and colors began to blur into a mirage of black and gray as the lights from headquarters faded behind me. It wouldn't be until later, and after walking up and down endless rows of cars that I would realize, the only way I was going find my vehicle on this night was to use the panic button.

I quickly jogged up to the vehicle then, happy to know that it was a small, silver Grand Am. I was thankful that I hadn't been stuck with the large van or truck. It's hard for a tiny girl like me to get used to driving large vehicles with so many blind spots. I wearily climbed into the little compact car and found my way over to the motel, which was just over two miles away.

As I was grabbing the room key from the lobby, I was surprised to find out that there were absolutely no hotel vacancies in Baton Rouge. The Red Cross had permanently rented out a block of rooms for the Operation, but the majority of hotels were simply filled with evacuees. It wasn't a temporary status either; it was going to be like this for months to come.

There were thousands now homeless and it was going to take months maybe even years for them to find new homes. It was a strange feeling after that when I noticed all the hotel signs with permanent "No Vacancy" messages posted outside.

It is amazing how much can change so quickly after such a devastating event such as a natural disaster. An entire city can be ripped apart and then sewn back together in an all-new haphazard attempt to survive on the means it is left with to operate on. It is something even history cannot help, when it is history itself, being made.

I pulled my car around to where my room was and snuck into one of the last spots available. As I closed my door softly, I coughed gently. This didn't seem to bother me though; I breathed in deeply, letting the warm night air fill up my lungs. I could already tell they were healing and that the cough itself was going away. It was a small dose of relief.

I pulled out my duffels and headed to the staircase that went up to the second level. I paused momentarily when I reached the first step and looked up into pitch-blackness. I glanced around me quickly when I realized there was no electricity in the stairwell.

All I could see were the stairs disappearing into a thick cloud of blackness. I hesitated for a moment feeling a little wary. There were no sounds around me and the silence seemed a little too quiet. I imagined a couple of large, muscled thugs just waiting for me at the top of the staircase wielding knives.

It was then that I reached down at my hip and realized my own knife wasn't there. We were told not to bring weapons down here and that we wouldn't need them. We were told that we would be safe and protected at all times. That was an oxymoron for sure!

It was only my first day here and I had already heard someone get shot, dealt with a bomb threat, and now faced a run-down motel with barely any working electricity and no security whatsoever. I was only 100 pounds and completely defenseless should anything happen. I felt so helpless out here in the midst of rampant crime and constant danger, with no way to defend myself. *I desperately needed sleep.*

I bravely took a deep breath and stepped into the darkness. I grabbed a loose handrail to the right and rapidly climbed to the second level. The weight of my luggage threatened to pull me backwards as I tried to climb the stairs fast, yet quietly. When I reached the top, I pulled out my cell phone to read the numbers on the doors.

Luckily, I saw that my room was right there around the corner to the right, and I eagerly slipped in with the help of my cell phone light. I locked and bolted the door behind me and checked the window locks before even setting down my luggage. I was thankful to see that the lights worked inside my room and didn't even pause to glance around.

Despite my exhaustion, I tore off my clothes and went into the bathroom. It was tiny! It was barely big enough to hold the toilet and the shower. There wasn't even room for a rug or anywhere to place your toiletries. I sighed and stepped into the bathtub. I turned the left knob all the way to the hottest setting, and was slightly taken aback at the dirty condition of the shower. The walls were covered with dirt, and I winced slightly as I felt slime beneath my feet.

Then, I froze as the "warm" water never turned warm. They didn't even have heated water! I could barely move as the icy water covered my body with frigid-like tentacles. I hurriedly squirted some body wash into my hands and tried to shower as best I could. My movements were slow, and the chilly water made it harder to move. Still, I was so thankful; for this was about the best anyone could get down here.

I did a double-take as I looked up to see a huge black spider slowly crawling down the dirty shower wall. On a normal day, I actually like spiders, snakes and catching frogs. They didn't even bother me too much, but having them accompany me in the shower was a little disconcerting. I decided to ignore it because at this point, I was just thankful to have a shower.

It wasn't home for sure, but after not sleeping, eating, or showering in two days...it almost felt like heaven, and I was thankful. I used the last bit of my strength to clean up and wash my hair. I quickly towel-dried, brushed my teeth, and threw on shorts and a tank top. I set my alarm for 6 a.m., flipped off the lights, and collapsed on the bed pulling my baby soft Tinkerbell blanket over me. I don't even remember closing my eyes...I was out.

SATURDAY, OCTOBER 1ST
MOTEL ROOM
6:00 A.M.

The shrill sound of my cell phone alarm roused me out of a deep sleep. I sighed, weakly opening my eyes as I tossed back the blankets. After sleeping so soundly, it took me a few moments to remember where I was. *Baton Rouge!* I remembered that I had to be back at Headquarters at 7:00 AM, and I didn't want to be late on my second day here.

I grimaced as I felt a sick, twisting pain in my stomach and my sudden attempt to get up backfired. I rolled my eyes in frustration as I recognized the pain of emptiness and hunger. At this point, I couldn't even remember the last time that I had eaten a meal. My trip so far hadn't been easy and every spare moment I had been settling into the routine of my obligations on this Operation.

I didn't have any snacks with me so I desperately made a pot of coffee. In between bouts of nausea, I forced myself to take several sips, frowning at the bitterness. I remembered the warning about contamination and prayed then that the water wouldn't make me sicker. I then felt a strange wave of weakness, and stood motionless as the coffee cup clattered to the floor.

Several violent flip-flops churned in my stomach and I felt myself about to lose my stomach again. I put my hand over my mouth and rushed into the bathroom falling to my knees, vomiting once again into the toilet.

I walked quickly back to the bed, collapsing for a few moments trying to regain a little strength. I took a quick shower again and shivering lightly, pulled on khaki shorts and a white tee. I tried not to look at the pale face staring back at me in the mirror, completely ashen white from being sick. *I looked awful!* I pulled my hair back into a ponytail, sticking a baseball cap on in a quick attempt to look presentable.

I grabbed my keys and headed back to Headquarters. I was supposed to report in at 7:00 AM. I would make it just-in-time.

When I got there though, I knew my first priority was to get something in my stomach. If I didn't do that next, I would be too sick to work and would have to be sent home. I couldn't let that happen. I wanted to help so badly and I knew I had a purpose in being here. I just knew it.

After the awful incident that morning, I truly started to realize that <u>if you want to help others, you have to help yourself first.</u> I would have to learn to discipline myself to eat and drink constantly on an Operation such as this, if I was going to be strong and healthy enough to last through it. We were very limited here with options for food, and it made it that much harder to eat healthy as we normally did back in our hometowns.

HEADQUARTERS
7:00 A.M.

I walked quickly up to the security post and flashed my Red Cross ID badge gaining entrance to the facility. I did a quick stop-off at the Oasis grabbing a bottle of water and a Pepsi. I was disappointed to find that there were no salt crackers available. All they had was a table filled with breakfast snacks including donut holes, breakfast bars, fruit, nuts, pop-tarts and more. That would only upset my stomach more!

I paused to ask the guy behind the counter if he had any crackers. I explained that my stomach was upset and needed something bland to eat. It was in that moment that once again I felt God's hand over me. The guy smiled and reached over to a small filing cabinet behind him and pulled out a long red box of saltine crackers and handed them to me.

"I don't know where these came from," he said, "but you're welcome to have them if you want."

I didn't care where they'd come from at this point. They could've come from the planet Mars for all I cared. I smiled in appreciation offering a sincere nod of thanks as I took the crackers. I hurriedly took my stash into the main room back to the Safety and Security Department.

Being the only young girl on the team, green-eyed and blond...I was welcomed with a swarm of hearty "good mornings" from the rest of the male crew. I smiled weakly and headed over to a chair to work on my crackers and water. I slowly started to feel better, and more importantly, I started to feel stronger as I ate.

The Lieutenant Colonel came up to me just then and asked me if I would go set up the digital photo ID department. Because of my experience with digital photography, I was being placed in charge of creating ID badges for all incoming volunteers today. I took the camera and printer over to the ID department where the laptop was already plugged in.

I quickly set up the equipment and typed in a special password to open the ID badge software. Once I finished setting up, I headed back to Safety and Security for our 8 o'clock briefing.

Our 8 o'clock briefings were protocol and would become the first part of our day. It was basically about 20 minutes set aside to update the SAS personnel on the latest Safety and Security developments, needs and changes on the operation.

After we were updated on the operation, they handed out our daily assignments and bosses for the day. Each person(s) was placed under the leadership of a more experienced individual. I was still under the leadership of the Lieutenant Colonel, and was assigned to creating ID badges.

All of the new incoming volunteers that were processed through Headquarters had to have a special Hurricane Katrina ID badge made before being sent out to their permanent assignments; to include their name and enlistment termination date. This was a way to keep track of all current volunteers and be able to replace the volunteers in a systematic manner.

In between the groups coming and going, I was asked to design a few databases for the Lieutenant on his laptop and put the entire network of our personnel into one system. The entire state of Louisiana had been divided into nine quadrants; each quadrant identified a Red Cross station in each disaster area.

We were having a problem with consistency. Our group in Safety and Security was new, having just arrived on the Operation and there was still no system in place to keep communication between Headquarters and all of our networks throughout Louisiana. With these databases, we would be able to track, update and correlate our Safety and Security missions!

I feasted the entire day on the saltine crackers, water, and soda, which slowly strengthened my body as I worked the camera. I began to enjoy tricking people into making them smile because for the most part, the groups were older individuals, who were not interested at all in having their picture taken. This wasn't meant to be a sad operation though. We were here to help people, and it was okay to be happy about it. <smile>

I was restacking the printer with blank ID badges when the Lieutenant appeared in front of me.

"Rose, were you able to create the Quadrant Database yet?"

I raised an eyebrow and smiled, "Sir, I completed that about five hours ago."

He paused for a moment taken aback and couldn't say anything. He raised his eyebrows as he thought for a moment.

Finally he spoke, his head cocked at an angle in surprise.

"Thanks, Rose...you have definitely surprised me."

I smiled getting back to my work. I think it was at that moment the Lieutenant realized that despite my young age, there was a competency about me that he could rely on. Being able to rely on someone was something that didn't necessarily come with age, but rather with the right attitude and determination. That meant a lot on this Operation when most individuals were scrambling around, completely frazzled while trying to handle one crisis before the next one occurred.

Being able to depend on someone, especially someone you barely knew, to accomplish and accurately complete any task needed…was in all reality, very hard to come by, almost impossible to find on this Operation. I personally was the type of person that took the initiative to just make things happen.

I didn't depend or rely on anyone else to help or assist me because I couldn't expect him or her to get it done. I always found it easier to accomplish something if I just did it alone. Working hard and efficiently accomplishes a lot. Waiting around for someone else to do it or for someone to guide you through it, rarely accomplishes anything.

I sensed a great lack of leadership on this Operation because there were so many different departments striving to accomplish so many different things, yet there was no common link that tied us all together. When this happens, then you have a trillion bosses and very few workers. We didn't need bosses, we needed one leader to facilitate and network the departments together.

On top of that, the standard changeover rate for personnel was every three weeks. That included the bosses and managers changing over every three weeks too. This meant that we constantly had new people coming in, not having a clue as to what was happening, and then trying to run a department on the perchance that they'll be able to pick up where the last person left off. This was really no one's fault but rather a simple weakness that would only be brought to light after a disaster of this magnitude.

The question was: would this fallibility change or only get worse? That is what scared me. Hurricane Katrina had dealt a crushing blow to this part of the country, it wasn't a simple fix, and it wasn't going to go away or get better without a lot of hard, hard work.

I realized it was up to those of us that realized this weak link, to step up to the plate and make things better. We would have to find ways to carry on the mission in the midst of the changeover, and also facilitate better communication between departments.

I am proud to say that by the time I would leave this Operation, I would be able to see these changes take place and a system take into effect which would help make this Operation a lasting success.

It wasn't anyone in particular's fault with all of the confusion. But really, what more could you expect when you pull over 20,000 random people from 50 different states and throw them together and say, "Help get Louisiana back on its feet!" My God, the madness! Only a miracle could facilitate an operation of that magnitude.

Half of the people sent down here had never even seen a disaster before, let alone the devastation they saw when they came here. Most people didn't even know how to handle or deal with it, period. Others had never been in supervisory positions and now found themselves placed into one. Some used the power just for fun, some even abusing it, while others had no clue what to do with it or how to handle it.

Even more, volunteers would find that the emotional duress of the operation would be too much to take and they would eventually have to return home early. There were even a lot of people that came down here to play, to escape, or to find adventure.

Actually, a lot of people came down here just because they could and thought it would be exciting to be on the frontlines of a major event in America's history.

And others, others came down here just for the curiosity of the event. It really shocked me to see all of this. It came to be very hard to find someone that just wanted to help!

SUNDAY, OCTOBER 2ND
HEADQUARTERS
8:24 A.M.

After my 8:00 briefing, everyone dispersed off with their assignments in hand. I was left standing alone. I turned around startled to hear my name being called. It was Lieutenant Williams, my boss. Having a boss that was in the military always kept me on my toes, and I constantly strived to make sure that I didn't disappoint him.

My heart started pounding deep in my chest as I walked slowly over to where he stood. I hoped to God that I wasn't in trouble, but in this moment, I was sure that I had done something wrong. I racked my brain trying to think of what I could have done, anything...? There had to have been something because I was the only one that hadn't gotten an assignment for the day.

I swallowed thickly as he said, "Have a seat."

I sat down feeling a different "sick to my stomach" take over me and gathered up the courage to look Lieutenant Williams in the eyes. He paused for a moment, his face unmoving, militaristic if I may say in its seriousness. I blinked rapidly, my eyes darting off, briefly breaking the intense stare.

"Rosemary," he said stopping for a quick, dramatic moment, "Are you ready?"

I stopped. I think that is the moment my eyes got really big. He'd used my full name! You were always in trouble when someone did that!

Ready?
Ready for what?
For war?

For peace?
To go home?
Now I was really confused!

"Umm Sir," I stuttered, "Ready for what?" I eagerly awaited his next words.

"To go out in the field?" he said matter-of-factly.

I think that is when my mouth dropped open. *Go out in the field?* Wow that was a huge compliment to me, being the only girl there.

Going out in the field meant anything from doing inspections, investigations, perimeter security, damage assessment, to security checks. Something that only trained officers, firemen, or law enforcement agents would be doing, or so I thought. I didn't really know what he meant.

"Umm…what do you mean Sir?" I asked. I needed to know more. There was no way he wanted me, a little 100 lb. girl to go out in the field, potentially swamps and woods, alone, to do Safety and Security missions.

"Rosemary, you have shocked and amazed me with your competency and hard-working attitude. You have superseded my expectations for what I originally expected out of you and your skills could greatly be used in the field." He paused for a moment as if pondering a thought.

"I need someone like you, if you are willing, to be ready to leave on a moment's notice to go out in the field on miscellaneous missions as need be. You will always be alongside a police escort and then report back to me."

I took in a deep breath and let it out slowly. *Okay so this made a little more sense. I thought he was asking to station me out in the field working on missions that most of the police officers were doing. Rather, he wanted me to do a job that no one else would be doing, one of demand and need, and one he felt I was competent enough to do. Wow!* That made me feel good.

I didn't even know all of the details at this point, but I began to feel a deep sense of excitement creep into my bones at this surprising inquiry.

I felt a small sense of accomplishment after only being on my third day of the operation, to be asked to take on greater responsibility. I would find out soon that this wouldn't be the first time it would happen. I appreciated the fact that Lieutenant Williams had noticed my hard work, and had enough faith in me, and my abilities to do so.

"Yes Sir, I'm ready," I smiled in relief. Ready for what exactly, I didn't know, but I was ready.

"Well then you're going to need some new clothes," he said again shocking me.

"Oh…ok?"

"Your first mission is tomorrow and you'll be out in the swamps and woods. You will need long pants, hiking boots or tennis shoes, long shirts etc. You can go now to pick up supplies. The Academy across the street should have everything you need." Lieutenant Williams explained.

When I had to been briefed at the Red Cross Chapter in Michigan on what to bring to Louisiana, we had been told to bring light, summer clothes. Pants had been discouraged because of the intense Southern heat, and hiking boots had definitely not been on the list. I guess when you think about it though, it was certainly hard for an office a thousand miles away to truly know what to expect on a mission operating all the way in Louisiana.

Even more, most volunteers were stationed near a client shelter. I had expected to be at one of those. At a client shelter, a temporary home for evacuees, the volunteers worked in or alongside a building and had no use for field clothes. It was all good though. I enjoyed the fast-paced environment at Headquarters and was definitely able to keep up with the constant changes. Multi-tasking was my element and anything short of it was too simplistic for me.

I pulled out a small notepad and pen and took down a list of items Lieutenant Williams said that I would need. I glanced up quickly as a sudden thought hit me.

"How will I protect myself?" I blurted out. I wanted some sort of protection! I didn't know what I'd be up against out there! *Remember the murder?*

"Yes, you should pick up a knife. They have a weapons section at the Academy. Make sure it is legal length and can be holstered on your belt and inside of a closed case." He added.

I breathed a sigh of relief when he said that. Being able to carry a knife was not only a handy weapon but also a very useful tool when you are out in the woods. Most of the volunteers in our department currently wore knives or holstered a gun. Most already did so back at home on their normal jobs and had simply carried on the procedure here.

"Alrighty," I said standing up. "I will go pick up the supplies I need and then report back to you."

"Sounds good Rose," Lieutenant Williams said winking at me. He got up and returned to work on his laptop as I gathered my keys to go pick up my supplies.

THE NEGOTIATION
2:35 P.M.

I returned to Headquarters about an hour and a half later after buying supplies and getting a bite to eat at a Burger King on the corner. It was the first "real" food I'd had since Michigan, and I ate every bit of it.

Perspiration beaded on my forehead as I stopped to pass through Security at the Headquarters entrance. It was about 92° today and the air came in heat waves that felt like a sauna. My long blonde hair clung to the back of my neck soaked in perspiration. I could feel the sweat dripping down my chest from beneath my navy polo and the bright sunlight made it difficult to see.

I was cleared to go inside the facility and quickly entered through the chain link luggage area, passing through the main glass door that opened into Headquarters. The door had just swooshed closed behind me when out of my peripheral vision I noticed a loud commotion to my left. I heard loud yelling and a heavy crash.

Back in Safety and Security, it was my job to help and assist in making sure Headquarters was safe...even if I was just a girl. Since I was part of that department, I had an obligation to help, I thought quickly.

I heard another shout and I hoped something bad wasn't about to happen. Acting inconspicuous, I paused momentarily to pull my hair back into a ponytail, using the motion to take in the scene just ahead of me. A sturdy, tall man approximately in his 50s, was waving his hands violently and smashing them into the wall. He uttered loud curses and threats all the while gesturing furiously at the group surrounding him.

I counted about five cops, two military persons, and most of the Safety and Security department closing in on him. I didn't notice a weapon on the man but could instantly sense the instability of his mind. His composure seemed calm for a moment then just as quickly switched to erratic and violent at the merest slip from one of the security personnel trying to get close to him.

Luckily, the scene was in the long entranceway that led into the main Headquarters area and not in the Main Department area itself. At least here there were only about 25 people working, compared to over 100 with in the main area. *That was one good thing!* I would have to pass through the commotion in order to get through to my department and started to contemplate my options.

Just then, one of the police officers noticed me and pulled away from the cluster surrounding the crazy man to come over to me. His name was Bill and he worked in Safety and Security with me.

"Rose," he said softly, pulling me discreetly to the side.

"We need your help," he started out, "We have a situation here and no one can get this man out of the building. We have the military and the police surrounding him and he keeps threatening the facility if they dare to make a move."

"How did he get in?" was my first question.

"He just barged in here past the guards and started yelling out threats."

"Who is he?" I asked.

"He actually came down as a Red Cross volunteer and was stationed at "Our Lady of Mercy" shelter. Then all the sudden, he went ballistic with the Shelter Manager. He's been on an immense amount of medication and drugs, and he's upset now because the Red Cross asked him to leave and return home because he was getting into fights with other volunteers and threatening the Shelter Manager.

"And why is he here?" I questioned.

"He got upset when he heard the orders for him to be sent home, so he found away over here to Headquarters trying to threaten us and retaliate because he doesn't want to leave."

"And so I'm assuming that the police and military have been unsuccessful in trying to get the man to leave the building, and at least be able to deal with the situation outside before he hurts someone in here?" I quickly gathered out loud.

"What is he threatening? Does he have a weapon?" I continued on.

"He's trying to get past the police barricade to get into the Main Department area to wreck havoc in there. Because of his medical condition and medication issues, it really complicates the situation. Clearly from the way he's talking, his mind is unstable and he can't think or act rationally. So we really aren't sure what he's capable of, and can't get close enough to frisk him for weapons."

"How did he get on the Operation?" I asked confused.

"You're asking me," Bills said with a shrug.

I cringed as the aggressor smashed his fist into the wall again, screaming in anger. It was interesting to note how the 25 people or so stationed in the room kept their heads down and tried to pretend like they were working.

"But Rose, you seem to have such a way with people," Bill whispered interrupting my thought. "I don't know how anyone could get upset with you, let alone argue with such a tiny, sweet girl."

"Bill, you can't be serious," I whispered back. *He had to be out of his mind!*

"You can't really be asking me to try to negotiate with a hostile aggressor where the police and military have failed! I am not a law enforcement agent! I don't have any experience or credentials to do anything that you guys can't do!"

I paused swallowing hard.

"I am not trained!" I repeated. "I don't know anything about a hostile negotiation." I continued.

I pressed my lips tight together. I wasn't scared by any means...just utterly shocked that I had just been asked to be a negotiator. *Me! Didn't you have to have a degree or something for that?*

"Bill, you can't be..." my voice trailed off as another fist smashed into the wall.

"Rose, I'm serious. I've seen you work with people here. Everyone smiles when they are around you, they can't help it. You encourage everyone here and always make others feel better in some way. You are amazing!"

I raised my eyebrow at him.

"C'mon, we are desperate, will you please at least give it a try? Otherwise, we are going to have to take him down forcibly, handcuff him and throw him in jail. That would create a huge scene worse than this, and we don't want anyone to get hurt."

"Bill, I will do whatever you ask me to, I just don't want to disappoint you." I said quietly.

"C'mon, it'll be fine." He said pulling me over to the cluster of activity.

I pulled away from Bill almost instantly before we reached the group, slipping into my act. I didn't have a moment to think about what I was going to do or say, so I slowed my pace for a moment. I knew that if this was going to work at all, I would have to act as if I wasn't part of Safety and Security or associated with any of the law enforcement agents.

Even though I didn't know the entire situation, I knew enough to take a stab. So far everyone had failed in getting the aggressor to willingly leave the building and right now, that was top priority. I pulled my ponytail out letting my long blonde hair hang free. I didn't want it to seem as if I was uptight or strict. I took off my Red Cross ID badge and slipped it into the back pocket of my jeans. I looked like an innocent, harmless, young woman then.

As soon as I came up to the group, it was as if the Red Sea had parted. The cops and military stepped back several feet giving the aggressor and I several feet of space. They still kept a tight circle around us, prepared in an instant to take action, should the man attempt to lay a hand on me. I wasn't wearing a weapon at this point. I was completely defenseless to be honest.

But it was in that moment, that a deep calm swept over me as I quickly began to put myself in this man's shoes. Common sense told me that barging up to him and ordering him to leave the facility would only make him more upset. The police had already tried that route and they had clearly been unsuccessful.

This man had come in here with the intention to attack, to punish, to hurt, and to take out his anger on us. What he felt now though, was a victim himself. Yes, it sounds crazy...how could the bad guy become the victim? Well with the force and potency of how cops and military personnel are used to operating, there is usually no cool or calm collectivity about it. It is usually a cold, stiff order to be followed, or punishment would immediately ensue.
   This man didn't like to be told what to do, let alone ordered what to do. He didn't like having just one option, or else. And, judging from the instability of his mind, I would bet money that I was right on this one. Not only that, but from the little I knew about this situation, the man seemed to be running from something.
   He was very desperate to not have to return home, and almost seemed to be using the Red Cross as an escape. And I had learned a long time ago that the expression of anger is simply the fear of being unable to cope with a situation. Nothing more than just exaggerated fear itself.
   I knew then what I would do. I had no clue if my intuition was completely correct, but I was certainly going to try. I ignored the stiff stares from everyone. The officers were watching every move of the situation, almost like a dog waiting to pounce on a stray cat. Waiting...just waiting for the man to make one wrong move, and give them the final reason to take him down.
   To this day, I do not know where my confidence came from in those next few moments, but it amazed even me how quickly I slipped into the mode of a calm, confident negotiator. Perhaps it was because I had no

choice, or perhaps it was because it was our only option.

I walked slowly up to the man letting him know I wasn't in a hurry. He ignored my presence and stiffened his back against the wall, leaned back further, and stared straight ahead.

Undaunted, I slipped to his left using my body to shield him from seeing the officers standing behind us in a half-circle, trying to make it seem as if it was just the two of us. I was trying to once again make it appear as if I was operating alone.

"Hey," I said softly. "My name is Rose," I said with a wide smile.

I was using a quiet enough tone that no one else could hear me in the room but him. He glanced quickly at me then resumed his blatant stare ahead, defiant in his posture and unmoving in his stance. I didn't pause in my introduction.

"Look, I don't know you or anything that is happening right now. I just want to say I know how you feel. You are standing here, and every police officer around is trying to tell you what to do. You have no options except one, and that is to leave. You are standing here because you just want someone to stop telling you what to do for once and to just listen."

He began to look at me then. I smiled softly looking him directly in the eyes showing that I had nothing to hide.

"May I ask your name?"

"Gunther." He muttered distrustfully.

"Gunther, I want to help you. But there is not much I can do with seven officers standing behind us. They are all upset with you for some reason, and I don't know the story exactly."

I paused for a moment gathering my thoughts.

"Even more, they are all telling you what you have to do without letting you speak. I know you have some things that you want to say, but there is no way anyone is going to listen to you in here."

"Gunther look at me," I said clearly.

"I don't know what is going on. All I know is what you need isn't inside here and therefore I can't help you."

He was looking at me now waiting for me to continue. I think he was surprised to hear that someone actually wanted to listen to him.

"If you want me to help you, you are going to have to walk out that door and get away from the police barricade. Then, you and I can talk and we will figure out a solution to help you."

That was it. I was done. I wasn't going to try to butter him up or coerce him to do anything. The cops had already attempted that. I just said what was on my heart and had done my best in just a few words to put myself in the man's shoes and to be a friend to him.

Just because he had a medical condition, or other personal issues, didn't mean that he was necessarily a bad person. Regardless, he was still a person, a human being, and he had feelings, emotions, and needs just like everyone else. And sometimes, with law-enforcement agents, they tend to use too much force and bullying to get their way or to implement the law because they are authorized to. But not realizing also, that sometimes it doesn't work like that in every situation.

I stepped back thinking it would take Gunther a little bit to make a decision. I wanted him to have a few moments to think alone, but I had barely moved back a step when he suddenly turned and hurriedly walked out the door heading outside the facility. My heart started pounding rapidly, and my mouth dropped open. I stood stock still as several officers trailed after him while the rest just stared in surprise, unmoving also. A few moments later, they all came over to me with hugs and patted me on the back expressing eager thanks.

Bill rushed back in from outside grabbing my hand.

"Rose, that was amazing! I knew you could do it! You really are something else. I still can't believe it!"

I just smiled. I was still surprised that my intuition had actually worked, and even more surprised that Gunther had willingly just walked out of the building. *I could not believe that had just happened!* I stood there not knowing what to do, but my smile still held strong.

"Rose, I have to ask you something else." Bill said quickly.

"Sure."

"Gunther is outside. He just broke down and is crying. You are the first person that he has listened to since he has been on the Operation. I want to ask if you will come with two police escorts in a van to take him to the airport."

Again, I raised an eyebrow in question. Now, I was being asked to do a police escort with an unstable aggressor. It seemed that with each passing moment on this Operation, a new surprise awaited me. I didn't even know if I should be surprised any more. Maybe this was normal on a relief operation. Maybe not, but I came here to help and at least I was being put to use!

"If you can just keep him talking, we can distract him enough to get him to the airport and then hand him over to the police there to get him on a plane. You have to make the decision because this is dangerous and I don't want to force you to do anything. However, I promise the other police officer and I will do our best to protect you from any harm or danger."

My adrenaline was pumping now. I didn't have to think too hard about it and I didn't feel I really had a choice. My goal down here on the Katrina Operation was to help in any way possible. I would do whatever I was asked.

"Yeah, I can do that." I answered confidently.

"Are you sure Rose? There is no telling what this man is capable of."

"No, I'm sure, I want to help."

"Ok, let's go." Bill said leading me outside.

Sergeant Martin rushed up just then saying quickly, "Gunther said he had to go to the bathroom. He's in the porter potty right now, but he's been in there for a while. I think he's stalling."

"He also might be committing suicide," I blurted out not thinking.

Bill quickly turned around to look at me.

"Yeah Sergeant, she's right. We need to try to get him to come out before he can do anything stupid."

"Rose, wait here." Bill said as he hurried over to the line of porter potties.

A large, unmarked white van pulled up just then, the driver having been carefully selected. He stayed in the van guarding it, and waited for us to get in.

I walked over to the van now parked right outside the porter potties and slid open the larger passenger door. I climbed in momentarily, shaking the driver's hand and introducing myself.

I slipped into the front seat while taking a look at the back seats. I figured I could sit up front in the passenger seat and Gunther could sit directly behind me. I could then sit with my back to the window, talk to him, and still have him in my peripheral vision at all times in case he attempted to hurt me or stop the vehicle. Sgt. Martin and Bill could sit in the seat behind Gunther. This would still allow Gunther some space, but also be guarded on all sides.

As I stepped out of the van, I turn to find Gunther, Bill and Sgt. Martin standing there.

"Hey Gunther," I said cheerily.

"Why don't you guys put Gunther's bag in the back while I help him figure out where we need to go." I said to Officer Bill and Sgt. Martin hinting wildly that I wanted a moment alone with Gunther.

Gunther pulled a set of headphones out of his bag and slung them around his neck.

"Hey, the driver here is going to take you and I to get the rest of your bags at the shelter where you were staying. We'll be able to talk on the way, okay?" I said in a nonchalant tone.

Gunther nodded slightly and climbed into the van and I followed hopping in the front. He then slipped on his music tuning me and everyone else out. *Well then!*

The two officers came around just then and slid into the seat behind Gunther pulling the large side door closed. The cop sitting directly behind Gunther had pulled out a small rope to use as a restraint, should Gunther make any sudden moves on any of us. I was shocked at the severity of the matter. Seeing the rope wrapped around the hands of the police officer made me realize just how serious this was.

As we were pulling away from Headquarters, I turned around to get Gunther's attention. He was once again staring straight ahead somewhere off in his own little world. I almost obnoxiously interrupted him, as a little kid would to their father saying, "So what kind of music are you listening to?"

He glanced over at me as if deciding whether or not to be mad at the intrusion, then mumbled something incoherently. I smiled and nodded as if I understood then asked, "Can I hear it?"

He paused for a moment then finally took off the headphone set and handed it to me. He was watching me now, waiting for my reaction as I slipped the headphones on. I don't know if I should have been surprised or not to hear Opera music playing. I was actually a little shocked. It was kind of strange and completely unexpected.

"I smiled back at him saying, "Umm, this music is relaxing!"

It was as if the lid came off the bottle then. After I handed him his headphones back, he never stopped talking.

"Yeah, they drown out the pain in my head. I have very intense headaches that the doctors can't cure."

And that would explain all the medication, I thought.

I then took a turn and shared with him two almost fatal car accidents that I had been in. The accidents had resulted in two consecutive concussions. Luckily on my end though, they had healed completely.

At this point, Gunther then felt he could relate to me and started spilling out his life story. By the time we had picked up his other belongings at the shelter and were heading out to the airport, I had found out that he'd just recently suffered some tremendous losses. He had lost his business, his wife had divorced him, and he had medical issues that the doctors couldn't cure. It was quite sad in fact, and after hearing his story, it made me feel better inside that I'd actually given him a chance to share it.

When it came down to it, he was left with nothing. And sometimes people just need someone to listen, someone to care because they feel very alone at the moment. And that would explain why Gunther didn't want to return home; he didn't really have anything at home to go back to.

But it also, was the very reason he couldn't stay here on the Operation. He wasn't stable enough in his mind or emotions to be able to handle the duress and difficulty of the relief work. He also would not be able to competently help others, when in fact he needed so much help himself.

It wasn't a mean decision on Safety and Security's part to send him home; it was simply the right decision. If you had taken the time to go through the training to get deployed, it should have only been done with the purpose to help. If the Red Cross was going to pay for people to travel from all over the country to go help on the Operation, it was going to be because the volunteers were going to help the victims, not to seek assistance themselves.

We arrived at the airport a few minutes later and successfully handed Gunther over to the police, who would make sure he made his return flight home.

It was amazing to see the change in temperament Gunther underwent from the time he was threatening Headquarters, to the time he stepped foot out at the airport entryway. He was calm, relaxed and it seemed almost as if all the fight was gone out of him. By the time the two SAS officers and I had gotten back in the van to return to Headquarters, a strong wave of exhaustion had fallen over me. The adrenaline disappeared at the finale of a mission completed.

I still think to this day of the shock felt at Gunther's willingness to leave the facility. Never in a million years would I have thought that he would listen to a young woman like me, yet he had and it had been a miracle. Should Gunther have decided not to obey the authorities, he would have been on his way to jail by now. Yes, it had been a successful mission.

THE PRESENT
6:29 P.M.

I was sitting at a small desk in the Safety and Security Department inside Headquarters writing up incident reports, when a gentleman from the Red Cross local volunteer booth walked up to me.

I paused in my writing to greet him, recognizing him from the front of the building where he was stationed and having greeted him several times on my way in and out of the building.

"Rose," he began with a smile, "I got you a present!"

I cocked my head to the side in question with a small smile on my face. *What? On a Disaster Relief site? They had presents here? And...why me?*

"A present?" I asked curiously.

"Yeah, he said handing me a small box wrapped with a simple plain white piece of copy paper and secured with a tan rubber band.

I was really curious at this point, and in an effort to not make the man feel nervous, I began to open the little present. As I was unwrapping the white paper, a small cutout from a magazine fell out. It was a photo of Anna Kournikova. I glanced up at the man raising my eyebrows.

"Yeah, I think you have striking resemblance to Anna..." the man said quickly. He averted his eyes briefly almost seeming shy.

I smiled to cover my confusion and peeked under the rest of the white paper, exposing a small gold box. I pulled it out gently realizing it was a tiny box of

Godiva chocolates. *Oh my! How wonderful! Godiva? No way! So so yummy!*

"Aww, thank you," I said gratefully. *How sweet! How did I deserve this? What had I done?*

"Where in the world did you find a box of Godiva chocolates and a magazine picture in the midst of a hurricane stricken land?" I blurted out in question.

The man just winked at me. *He must be an angel! What a sweetheart!*

"Thank you so much, you really made my day." I said humbly.

I do have to say, that moment was a special one for me. Never had I expected to receive a gift on the Operation or for someone to be thinking of me, yet in the late afternoon reprieve I felt a welcome wave of relief.

Here I was, working harder than ever, only thinking of what I could do for others, and here was a gentleman who was thinking of me; who wanted to say thank you. It was a ray of sunshine right in the midst of the stress and pressure of the Operation, the negotiation, everything and it brought a small dose of comfort. This proved that even in the midst of the storm and duress of saving lives, little things like surprise boxes of chocolate show that we can still be normal in the middle of such traumatic events.

It was the first time since my arrival that I had a taste of what life was like back home. It was a very different world down here. Yes, I was adapting just fine, but I hadn't forgotten either how things were supposed to be or what it felt like to know someone else was thinking of you.

"Rose, you always have such a bright smile on your face. I just wanted you to know how much I appreciate that. You just don't see smiles down here and you are changing that."

My eyes misted over as his words reached my heart. *I was changing Headquarters? Wow! I hadn't even realized that I had affected so many people already. The **power** of a **smile**? To actually **change** the world around you? That's amazing!* I thought. *I must never stop smiling!*

I reached up and gave the man a hug and murmured a sincere offer of thanks once more before he returned to his station.

It was so good to see someone else happy here. So many people were so stiff, cold and stressed that they had a hard time breaking a smile anymore. It was a welcome relief to know that someone else enjoyed being here also.

FIELD ORDERS
7:09 P.M.

Lieutenant Williams approached me just as I was closing up a file. Somehow I just knew that something important was up.

"Yes," I said smiling in greeting.

"Are you ready to go out in the field Miss Rose?" He asked folding his hands across his chest.

I took a deep breath before responding.

"Yes Sir. When do I leave?"

"Actually, you will be accompanying me tomorrow morning. We are heading up to Lake Charles to assess how bad the damage is from Hurricane Rita. We will also stop in De Ridder to secure and establish a Safety and Security network up there."

I was to accompany my boss, the Lieutenant Colonel? I was very excited to be asked to come along. It sounded like a very important mission.

"Meet me here at Headquarters at 7:00 a.m., we'll gather water and snacks and then head out into the field."

He bent down to make sure I caught his eye.

"Make sure you dress for the woods and swamps and bring plenty of bug repellent. We are going out in the boonies."

I swallowed thickly at his words.

"Yes Sir, I'll be here dressed and ready at 7 o'clock sharp."

The Lieutenant Colonel nodded and returned to his desk, leaving me there to ponder the words he'd just said. This would be the first time that I would be able to see the devastation left by the recent hurricanes. Hurricane Rita had hit the Western part of Louisiana just several days prior. Tomorrow we would be heading into quadrant nine, the newest quadrant, and the only one that wasn't yet set up or secure with the Red Cross presence.

As we would find out tomorrow, there would be a few other unexpected surprises as well.

MONDAY, OCTOBER 3rd
HEADQUARTERS
7:00 A.M.

I walked into Headquarters wearing a pair of dark jeans, a thick black T-shirt, tennis shoes, a baseball cap and sunglasses. Slung over my shoulder was a small blue duffel bag carrying bug repellent, water, snacks, gum, a flashlight, my clipboard, notepad, pen, camera, and a few other essentials. Tight around my waist was a black belt with my new knife strapped to my right side. My Red Cross Safety and Security badge hung loosely around my neck.

I met with the Lieutenant inside. We stayed for the 8:00 briefing then proceeded to load our supplies into his vehicle, a gray Ford escape.

I grabbed a stack of maps since I would be navigating and hopped in the front seat. Lieutenant Williams took the wheel and we headed out.

Our first stop was Lake Charles, which was approximately four hours away by car. There, we were to assess the damage left from Hurricane Rita and see if the Red Cross could do anything to help in that area. As far as we knew, Lake Charles wasn't terribly hit and was currently stable enough to not need Red Cross assistance.

We had sent out a scout a day or two prior to survey the damage, determine if the victims needed assistance, and see if the military had been able to set up rescue and recovery operations.

At the two of us made our way through long-wooded roads, surrounded by bayous with the occasional glimpse of alligators, some alive, some dead...we were unaware of the horror that awaited us at our destination.

MONDAY, OCTOBER 3rd
LAKE CHARLES
12:35 P.M.

As we were approaching our destination, the Lieutenant pulled off onto a service road several miles before to begin scouting out damage on the outer edges of the city. A huge billboard loomed ahead, with wind-whipped shreds hanging down in twisted tendrils. An empty face, a blank message, and a stark reminder of what had been before, was now completely torn away.

The trees started coming in thicker groves and hazy clouds filled the large expansive sky.

My eyes whipped back to the road as the car suddenly swerved to the left to avoid smashing into a huge uprooted tree, lying lifeless on the dark pavement. *Something wasn't right here,* I thought in that moment.

The Lieutenant slowed down to just 10 miles an hour to crawl around the debris-filled road. Thick branches were flung haphazardly into the fields and roadways and huge power lines hung precariously on a slant with their wires severed at the ends.

Lieutenant Williams was silent as he courageously guided the car through the aftermath of wind terror. I was confused as to why we'd just been told that there was no damage to Lake Charles, when here we could clearly see that there was. Unbeknownst to us, this was just the beginning.

Lieutenant Williams then turned to pull onto a side road that had several tiny houses. My heart skipped a beat as our vehicle rolled over a downed power line. I prayed fiercely that it wasn't a live wire. I breathed a sigh of relief as nothing happened.

"This isn't looking good." He said stiffly.

The Lieutenant then flipped the wheel in an attempt to turn our vehicle around, swerving onto a small makeshift ramp that served as a platform to cover a deep ravine below. I gasped as the Lieutenant overextended, throwing our vehicle off the edge of the platform!

I gripped the side of the door as our front two tires slipped off the edge, our vehicle hanging there for a few miraculous moments. I didn't move. I stared straight ahead still shocked that we were hanging off the edge of a ravine and that the slightest movement could push us over!

The next several minutes flashed by in a blur. I continued staring straight out the windshield wondering if my mere attempt to breathe would be enough to send us completely over the edge.

It is amazing how in mere moments one can slip from normal to life-threatening circumstances; it always reminds me to never take one second for granted. I felt completely helpless in that moment, knowing that for one, there was no one to help us, and two, we were completely stranded in the middle of nowhere.

All the houses here were abandoned, quickly having been evacuated just before the hurricane hit. It is hard to remember sometimes down here that we are the help, and when we are in trouble, there is no one to help us. It was with these thoughts that I prayed silently for a miracle.

There is no way with my body size that I would have the strength to push us off the edge and back onto solid ground. And, I highly doubted the Lieutenant could even do it himself. I slowly turned my head to the left glancing at Lieutenant Williams for his reaction. I caught his gaze and in that moment it was as if a silent message passed between us. No words were spoken as we both turned to move.

I gingerly cracked my door open, slipping down onto the platform. At the same time, the Lieutenant slid the car into neutral and opened his door. I crept around the side and back, quickly going over to where Lieutenant Williams hung outside the car with one foot on the brake and one foot on the platform. I adjusted my weight to match his as he slid out of the driver's seat onto the platform, and I quickly stepped up inside the vehicle, putting my foot on the brake.

The Lieutenant hurried around to the front of the vehicle cautiously keeping his feet planted on the platform while placing his hands on the front end of the car that was hanging precariously off the edge.

It was in that moment that he looked up at me through the windshield and gave me a quick nod. I quickly shifted the gearstick into reverse and began to abruptly rev the car into motion. The Lieutenant used the rocking motion to get a better hold on the SUV and used the momentum to push the vehicle backwards. *There is no way in heaven that this is going to work,* I thought frowning worriedly.

The front tires were spinning loudly not going anywhere. The smell of burnt rubber started to toast the air. Just as I was about to give up hope, the car suddenly lurched violently back, the front tires smacking loudly onto the platform. I breathed a sigh of relief as I cautiously backed the vehicle off the platform and back onto the road. My hands were shaking as I opened the driver's door to step down.

"Thank you Rose, you did a good job." The Lieutenant said walking up. "I'm really sorry about that, I had a hard time judging that one."

"It's ok," I said with a forced smile. Stuff like that happens. I was just thankful we were able to help ourselves get back on the road, because for a few moments there, I thought we were going to be stranded victims ourselves. Who knows how long it would be before we would have been able to find someone to trek through all the debris and downed power lines to get to us.

THE HARBOR
1:58 P.M.

We found our way back to the main side road we had started out on, and once again began painstakingly choosing our way around the downed trees, branches, and power lines. We headed down a little route that led to the harbor.

The sun was peeking through the clouds at this time and the dreary mood seemed to brighten a bit. I wasn't expecting anything bad here near the water. It appeared quite peaceful and serene as we approached with the sunlight bouncing off the deep gray ripples and a slight breeze was blowing.

We parked the vehicle just in front of the little beach area to head down to the water and inspect for damage or changes. A large bridge spanned to our left, held secure by huge cement pillars near the water's edge.

As soon as I slipped my sunglasses on, and closed the car door, a strong potent odor overtook my nostrils. *What was that? That's very strange! Why would the water smell so bad?* I walked slowly up ahead towards the water's edge, my boots falling heavily on the murky sand, discolored and muddy from the torrent of the storm.

My eyes froze for a moment when I realized that the sandy grass I was standing on was strewn with hundreds of drowned fish. There were big fish to little fish, even crawfish and crabs and other little sea critters. I could imagine in my mind then, the height of the storm surge viciously ravaging the harbor. It uprooted and tormented everything in its path and then receded at its own pace. It coldly left helpless amphibians to drown on the waterless ground, gasping for breath, until the air itself killed them.

The warm sunlight, muddy water and slippery breeze offered a horrid smell tinged with the smell of death itself. It was a very sobering moment as I just stood there taking in the scene. I took out my camera and snapped a few pictures for our records.

The fish mouths hung open as if in one final plea for help. I turned just then to gaze out across the water, inspecting the other parts of the harbor, when another surprising view hit me. On the right edge of the harbor there were a ton of little fishing boats smashed into the embankment and carelessly shredded into pieces. They just hung there as if waiting for someone to realize they weren't supposed to be like that.

I let out a deep sigh snapping another photo just as the Lieutenant walked up to me.

"You, ready?" He asked kindly.

"Sure," I said turning to head back to the vehicle.

"Rose, I think our scout was wrong." He said matter-of-factly.

"Yeah, I was thinking the same thing." I said. "It doesn't appear at all to be in recovery mode yet."

"I don't think anyone realized that Rita hit here, they are still so focused on Katrina." He muttered pulling back onto the roadway.

"I can't believe the Red Cross didn't even know about this. We need to be here helping!" I exclaimed worriedly.

THE CIVIC CENTER
2:31 P.M.

We began to enter the heart of the city now, and realized almost instantly that the city was without power. No street lights were working, all of the businesses were closed, and debris lay strewn all over the roadsides.

The buildings had large chunks just missing and tons of glass lay shattered over the streets and sidewalks from blown out windows.

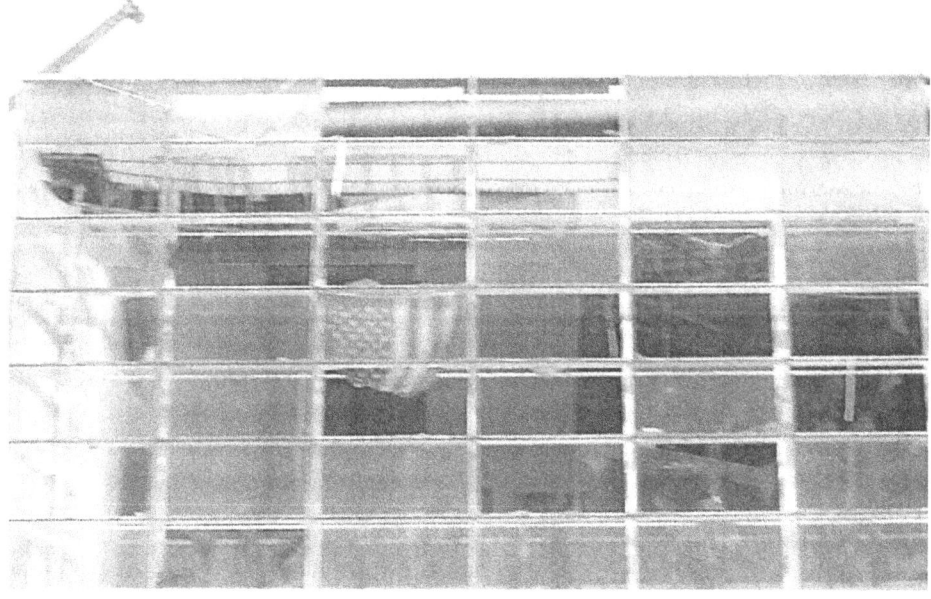

My eyes just clung to the wreckage...once again shocked and surprised. It was so sad and heartbreaking to see such a special city such as Lake Charles completely standing in ruins. It was without power, water, food, and completely devastated.

I could see people now walking through the rubble trying to find any belongings that had survived the storm. I then heard the Lieutenant on the phone calling Headquarters with our surprise findings. He quickly gave a summary of what we'd found so far and paused mid-sentence when we came upon the Civic Center up ahead, noticing a large military helicopter preparing to take off.

"Yeah, they are still doing rescue operations here!" He said angrily.

"Our informant was wrong! The city is completely devastated and we need to get the Red Cross up here now!

He hung up the phone openly agitated.

We inspected more of the city, taking more photos to bring back to Headquarters as proof. It was amazing to note that almost every single house lay crushed by a large oversized tree. It appeared as if not one had escaped harm.

Others lay trapped under downed power lines, or charred from recent fires. Many trees had been twisted apart from tornadoes, while others had just been completely uprooted from the storm.

The debris was intense. It was a thick mess of leaves, branches and trees all scattered together, leaving a sobering aftermath.

EATING IN THE FIELD
3:35 P.M.

After snapping a final few photos, we pulled back onto the main road. The Lieutenant drove for several miles and then decided to stop the car to take a quick lunch break. Today we would be feasting on MRE's (the military's famous packaged meals) and drinking bottled water and Gatorade.

It was definitely a change to go from being able to pick up fast-food at a Wendy's in Michigan, to coming down here to hurricane-stricken Louisiana where the lack of power, supplies, and contamination provided no source of reliable, safe or sanitary means of food or water in most locations. I wasn't complaining though.

I was never picky about food, just always thankful to have it. Even more, I had never had an MRE and was excited to try it. MRE stands for "Meal, Ready-To-Eat".

We gathered our lunch and hunkered down on a barren sidewalk to "cook" it. It fascinated me to no end to see how the MRE worked, even more, to find out what little surprises waited inside. It was like opening a Christmas present for me. You never know what you're getting until you open it, and I love surprises.

I was shocked even more when I pulled out a small brown bag of M&Ms...my absolute favorite candy! *Since when did the military put cute little treats like that inside? Weren't MRE's supposed to be gross and tasteless? Well, they must've come a long ways,* I thought as I watched my chicken simmer.

All you had to do to cook your meal was pour a tiny bit of water up to the waterline and it caused a chemical reaction that heated it up. It took about 10 minutes to cook, but the wait was worth it since I was completely starving. It was super yummy!

MY FIRST MRE

DE RIDDER, LOUISIANA
4:22 P.M.

After coordinating with the military and law-enforcement agents at the Civic Center on the needs and means to bring the Red Cross in to aid the city, we pulled out the map once again to head north to our final destination.

We were heading to De Ridder, a city just north of Lake Charles to check on our security operations there and make sure that the Red Cross shelter didn't need any assistance. It was our most recent shelter that had been set up and we wanted to make sure that they had all the support they needed from our department at Headquarters.

By the time we arrived, a deep exhaustion had already begun to sweep over me, and I was finding it hard to keep my eyes open. I tried to ignore the fatigue as I stepped out of the vehicle and pulled out my clipboard.

We were meeting with our Security Head, Tom to make sure everything was going okay, and to get him up to speed on the latest details of the Operation.

We had pulled into a tiny parking lot a couple of blocks from the shelter that we were inspecting, then headed over to meet our contact just a couple of cars down from where we had parked.

The warm air even in the late afternoon beckoned me and made me just want to sleep. We shook hands in greeting and headed over to a dilapidated building, empty and desolate, to have a short little meeting in private. Tom and the Lieutenant stood several feet from me already engrossed in conversation. My job at this point was to take notes of the meeting and document any changes or updates for us to take back to Headquarters. I was the data collector and began listening to the two rapidly exchange information.

I didn't want to be rude but I was having a hard time paying attention to their conversation because I felt faint and could only think of finding a place to rest. A few minutes later I started to swoon.

With the heat of the afternoon and the fatigue from all the adventures of the day, I was slipping into a state of exhaustion so deep that I realized I couldn't even stand. I slipped down quietly onto a low-standing porch to lean up against pole.

The windows behind me were completely covered with a thick layer of dust and I wondered when the last time anyone had set foot in building. I planted one of my feet on a broken step and the other in the sand below to try to support the jelly-like feeling in my legs, and I prayed that the wooden planks I sat on wouldn't break beneath my weight.

I set my clipboard to the side still trying to listen as the men talked. I coughed slightly as a swirl of dust rose and tickled my nose, and I didn't even think for a moment to beware of the Louisiana critters. I was almost too tired to care and certainly not awake enough to remember the warnings. Bad things can't happen when you're tired, right?

I was wiping the sweat from my brow when I happened to look downward. Out of the corner of my eye I noticed a rapid movement at my waist. My eyes froze in terror as I noticed hundreds of ants racing up my body, already covering both of my entire pant legs and waistline! I couldn't move for a moment trying to will away the horror of what I was seeing. *Fire ants!*

Fire ants! They bite, they bite, they bite! The venom from multiple fire ant stings could be fatal if it causes a severe enough allergic reaction! *It was an army attack!*

A fire ant army attack means that every single one of those ants would do their best to sting you as many times as they could and as quickly as they could, inserting their venom within their bite. They are very aggressive and very unforgiving. *Noooooooooo, this couldn't be!*

My fatigue was forgotten in that moment and I shot up like a rocket brushing the ants furiously off my clothes. My efforts accomplished nothing. There was too many of them! I had rested my feet on a large anthill of them! The men noticed me then thrashing awkwardly. They knew immediately what had happened.

"Rose! You can't get them off that way! You have to take off all your clothes or they will attack your whole body!" The Lieutenant shouted.

"Rose!" Tom shouted, "Run over to that building on the corner, that's the shelter! Go strip down in there! Hurry! Run!"

I didn't pause for a moment. My feet flew never resting long enough on the ground to even be considered a step. I ran feeling like a complete fool for having let down my guard even just for those few moments, but yet long enough to get me into trouble.

I prayed desperately that the ants wouldn't bite me, stomping my feet into the ground harshly as I ran, trying to shake them off. I had no idea if I was allergic or not to fire ants. I knew I was allergic to mosquitos but had no clue about fire ants. But if I was how long would it be before my airway swelled up and closed, and I couldn't breathe anymore?

I couldn't tell if I was being bitten because I was concentrating so hard on running. I came up to a one-way street and ran across rushing through a quick gap in vehicles, and ignored an angry honk behind me.

I flew into the building like a mad woman. *Where was the bathroom?* I'd never been here before and there were three separate halls in front of me. *What do I do?*

I was almost crying then in frustration but on a whim took the left hall knowing I had to try. I didn't want to strip naked in front of a large room of people and inwardly prayed that there was a woman's bathroom down this hall. Miraculously there was, and I rushed inside.

Immediately, I tore off my shirt, kicked off my shoes, my pants...literally everything...letting them fall crazily to the floor. I think I broke a record for undressing in the amount of seconds it took me to discard my clothing. I kicked it all aside and started brushing my arms and legs to knock off any of the ants that had snuck underneath my clothing. I couldn't see any, but I knew that I was going to feel their bite at any moment.

Luckily, most of the ants had been on the top of my clothes and since I had worn thick socks, tennis shoes and long pants, not even one had had a chance to penetrate to the skin yet. Even then, I kept wildly shaking my arms and stomping my legs. I then brushed off invisible ants off my skin not believing that I had just escaped a colony attack.

I climbed onto the toilet, planting my feet on the seat to get away from the ones crawling on the floor. I stood like that for a few moments with my hands braced on the stall wall catching my breath until I was sure that there were no more ants on me and that the threat of being bitten was completely gone.

I then gingerly picked up my clothes holding them as far away from me as possible and quickly stepped out of the stall. I roughly shook them out, not once, not twice, but many times. I shook them out so much I even put a clothes-dryer to shame. When I was completely sure all of the ants had been shaken off and smashed into lifeless spatters with the bottom of my tennis shoe, I slowly put them back on.

Even though the ants were gone, I was still waiting to get bitten. It was an imagined fear that perhaps one ant had gotten stuck in my pant leg and was just waiting to bite down.

I washed my hands in the sink and frowned at the haggard look on my face. If I had thought I had been tired before, the attack of the ants had topped the exhaustion with a feeling of complete lack of energy and lightheadedness.

FORT POLK
5:17 P.M.

Tom and Lieutenant Williams met me as I walked out of the bathroom to make sure I was okay. I smiled weakly, a little embarrassed at the incident and follow them around to the front of the building. We finished up our goodbyes in De Ridder, finding everything stable and running efficiently. All of our security measures were in place and all of our volunteers had been updated on all current operational stats.

The sun was starting to simmer at this point, pausing at the edge of the horizon in a waning ball of orange and yellow. The Lieutenant and I climbed back into the SUV and headed for one more stop before returning to Baton Rouge. We needed to fill up on gas.

Unfortunately, all of the gas here had been contaminated from intense flooding, so we were forced to seek higher ground at Fort Polk, another half hour or so away.

TUESDAY, OCTOBER 4th
NEW ORLEANS
8:40 A.M.

Today I was so excited. My assignment was taking me into New Orleans alongside Officer Grant. I'd heard so many stories of the city and the aftermath, and I was eager to see it for myself. We were going into the city to check on our previous evacuee shelters there and survey the damage. These shelters had all been evacuated once Katrina had hit and we wanted to make sure our presence was still known.

We were also going in to reconnect with the police and National Guard and make sure a communication network was reestablished with Headquarters. There were two individuals that worked in Media Relations (reporters) that wanted to follow us to document the recent changes.

The Lieutenant had requested that alongside our reconnaissance efforts, that I photograph all of our findings. I was always looking for a chance to snap a picture, so the request was met with great enthusiasm.

Officer Grant and I quickly said our goodbyes and cleared the building. The media would be following us in a separate vehicle. Both parties designated one driver and one navigator. Unfortunately for me, I was designated as the navigator. I am the queen of getting lost, even in my home state! I smiled inwardly. *This should be interesting!*

I could only imagine my mom laughing at me right now because she was always the one I called to bail me out when I couldn't find my way somewhere. It was kind of ironic for sure that I was the one who was chosen to read the map! Still, I can't say (me) driving into unknown territory would have been much better.

We quickly loaded up supplies into the back of Officer Grant's rental Jeep Cherokee and hopped into the vehicle to begin our trip. He made sure to bring enough food and water to last the day because there was nothing sanitary or even available in New Orleans.

The first thing Officer Grant said was, "Ok Rose, before we leave we have to put on some tunes!"

I laughed thinking to myself, *oh no, he's at least double my age…this is going to be torture!* But, it was his car and his music, so I just nodded and smiled. I hoped the car ride into New Orleans wouldn't be too unbearable. <smile>

He ended up putting on some older country that I was unfamiliar with, but he seemed to enjoy it and that was enough to make me happy. I pulled out my stack of maps trying to pinpoint how to get us out of Baton Rouge and onto a more direct route into New Orleans.

Because I don't use maps that often, let alone navigate at all, I peered intently at the mass of intertwining roadways in front of me as if to appear that I was familiar with map reading. I didn't want to admit that I didn't have a clue what I was doing because I didn't want to seem like I was incompetent or incapable of doing what the Lieutenant had entrusted me to do. I figured that I would try my best and that was all I could do.

I was happy that I had been assigned so many different jobs since my first day here. I felt that there must be something I was doing right which made me feel like I was finally starting to make some sort of difference here. I always try to go above and beyond in my life and coming down here on the Operation, I just wanted to make the Red Cross proud of my work, and to be some sort of inspiration to those who had lost their smile from their severe losses.

It is nice to be able to help someone find a new home or provide a meal for them, but there's nothing greater that we can do for another then being able to inspire them to believe again in hope. And as long as there is hope, there is faith, and as long as there is faith, there is a future.

Luckily for me, Officer Grant was somewhat familiar with getting onto Route 10 that would take us out of Baton Rouge and into New Orleans, and he made a haphazard guess that put us right on track. By the time we would get into the city, we would find that the map would be of no use anyways since all of the street signs had blown away in the hurricane. *Literally!*

The sun was shining and our conversation drifted off as the music began to take over our thoughts. The calming relaxation of the warm, sunny air, and tree-filled roadways with their leaves flapping in the breeze had a soothing effect. It was a well needed moment to relax and drink in the peace of having no current pressing responsibility of life or death action.

I gazed along the side of the road deep in thought hoping to see alligators sunbathing, sleeping, or moving in any way for that matter. We don't have alligators in Michigan, so it stoked my curiosity and gave me something nonchalant to focus on.

As our drive continued on, the scenery around slowly began to change. I scooted up in my seat to get a better view. Instead of trees standing upright, we begin to see split, slashed or uprooted ones. Power lines once again were torn and strewn carelessly over the landscape. Debris was scattered and mixed among it all and huge broken branches hung precariously over anything still standing.

A deep sense of trepidation began to fill me then. It was a sort of impending doom like I was heading into the mouth of a dragon. It was a dragon of devastation, destruction and a delicate demise of ruins.

I was so unsure of what to expect when we had begun this trip, but now my smile faded and my face fell into look of grim sadness. *Would there be dead bodies still lying around? Would there be any buildings left standing? Would there be any people milling around? Would there be any stray dogs wandering the streets abandoned and alone? Would there be anything left?*

My mind started sifting through the possibilities of what I was about to see and I tried to not expect the worst. I kept my mouth quiet in respect for the destruction that we were passing by, not wanting to spoil the silence with invasive questions.

I pulled out my digital camera to take several shots as we headed closer to the city. I almost felt guilty snapping photos of the devastation as if I was an intruder, for in a sense I was. I was an outsider, an invader, someone from over 1,000 miles away walking into the pain, loss and sorrow of complete obliteration from a Category 5 Hurricane.

Katrina wasn't kind upon her arrival to the United States. She was heartless, vicious, and her landfall took only mere minutes to completely ruin the lives of the Louisianians, and all they had lived for or had ever known. Just like that it was gone; their livelihood that went back generation after generation. In the end they were left with nothing. Then, here I was driving into the aftermath of the horror. It was a strange feeling inside, as the city of New Orleans loomed closer.

As we began our passage across a long, undamaged bridge, I turned slowly to the right to peer at the water flowing peacefully underneath its smooth arches. It was a strange calm following the storm. The water appeared to be lulling quietly in a strained melody of music.

It was just a moment longer when I realized that my initial observation had been a deceitful mirage. Just up ahead I noticed something large and unnatural to a body of water floating by.

It was a pale blue house, half submerged in the water surrounding it. Shredded floorboards stood straight up in the air as if pointing a furious finger at the sky, angry for ruining its very existence. *Oh no!*

Just seeing someone's past home floating by, abandoned and lost, made my heart sad. I leaned out the Jeep's passenger window to take several pictures and several questions began to go through my head. *Who have lived here before? What had they strived so hard to gain just to have it stolen from them the day Katrina hit? Where were those people now? Had they survived the hurricane or had the tragic storm taken them to?*

We kept on driving over the bridge noticing that the swells of water were raised abnormally high around the submerged pillars. I snapped several more pictures capturing moments that would mark our history for a lifetime.

As we got closer to our New Orleans destination, Officer Grant asked me to take out the map again. Prior to our early morning departure, we had plotted six different target points for our route today. All we had to do now was find our way to the first destination point and maneuver our way through the streets in a straightforward direction after that.

Larger buildings began to appear as we began to enter the outskirts of New Orleans.

Even the height and strength of the building shown here did nothing to thwart the hurricane's vicious winds sending huge shards of glass twisting through the air.

Our windows were still rolled down as we headed off the highway onto a main side street. As Officer Grant made another turn onto Claiborne Avenue, a deep pungent odor caused me to almost choke in mid-air. It was a smell that was clearly definable. It was a smell that spoke of death, deterioration, mold, wet, garbage, sewage and waste.

I quickly noticed that it made breathing difficult. I reached up to cover my mouth with my left hand in an effort to quell the bile rising up from my stomach. I glanced briefly at Grant and noticed he was fighting the same thing. I didn't say anything then.

I turned around for a moment to see if the Media Relation's group was still following us and frowned slightly when I saw no one behind us. *They must have decided to venture off on their own or perhaps they got lost...*

I turned back around and noticed just up ahead a weary looking man wearing a white facemask, guiding the thin flow of traffic. The moment I saw the mask covering the man's mouth and nose, I felt a flash of fear slip over me. *If the man had to wear a mask to breathe the outside air, shouldn't we be wearing masks too?*

I thought for a moment and remembered having heard something about the mask situation in New Orleans. Just several weeks after the hurricane had hit, there had been new reports that had come in of workers who had already begun to lose the hair on their arms and heads from the mold and contamination in the cleanup.

The intensity of all of the escalating environmental factors that were swarming out of control were not just apparent on the television, they were even more apparent standing several feet from you, I thought with a sickening feeling.

I could see the abandoned cars pushed into the median, coated with salt from the storm's waters. A few moments later I was surprised to feel a small smile play on my face as I noticed a traffic light lying on the ground yet still working. It was ironic to see that the one's still standing were not working, but this one on the ground was! *Of course!*

Even here the Red Cross presence was apparent. Huge signs were taped to poles and trees having guided evacuees several weeks earlier toward a nearby shelter where they would have been able to find refuge.

Road signs such as stop signs, U-turn signs, and one-ways had fallen, flipped upside down, faced the wrong way or completely disappeared. It was quite a frustrating venture the moment we realized that most every single street sign had blown away in the hurricane winds.

Even more unfortunate was the fact that we were not equipped with a GPS system that would allow us to navigate on our route for this trip.

Still having the role of navigator made my efforts to guide us through the maze of intertwining streets of the city, a city in which I had never been to before, cause me to feel like a fool.

I was scared to say turn left, hoping it was Freret Street, or whatever street was next on the route, only to run into countless other obstacles such as current road construction, debris cleanup crews or even completely impassable roadways from downed trees or power lines.

I kept praying inside that Officer Grant would ask me to drive and somehow figure out the navigating. I felt completely useless and worthless knowing that it was up to me, and the map, to still find our route while Officer Grant focused on just staying on the road with all of the debris.

Above was our first stop. This building had actually been a Red Cross food distribution center right after the hurricane hit. Grant pulled over to the side of the road deciding to talk with a couple of policemen who were guarding the entrance to the parking lot.

As we stepped out of the vehicle, we were slightly taken aback by an even more vile smell than what we had noticed before. It was so horridly potent and thoroughly disgusting that my stomach began to cramp in tight twists of protest. The saliva disappeared from my mouth and I felt the few contents left in my stomach making its way upward.

Sweat beaded on my forehead and the blistering heat from the smoldering sunlight caused my head to spin wildly. My body felt strangely faint and I was having a hard time swallowing. I weakly turned and grabbed my clipboard, repositioned my knife in my hip where it had slipped a little, and followed Officer Grant over to the gate where the policemen stood.

As we were greeting each other and flashing our Red Cross badges to identify our purpose, I suddenly knew I was going to be sick. I was completely embarrassed for not even being able to mumble the word "hi" but rather "do you guys have a bathroom?" I had this sick, helpless look on my face, my right hand on my stomach and an awkward effort to hold my breath.

The officers didn't seem too happy to see us and kind of just stood there with stiff stares. I was a little irked too because my job was to help gather information on our shelters, take detailed notes and snap clear photographs and here I was running into the bathroom again.

One of the officers pointed behind him, ignoring my presence and turned back to hear what Officer Grant had to say.

I didn't wait to say thanks and hurried over to where the officer had pointed. Much to my surprise, the bathrooms turned out to be a row of three yellow rank-smelling porter potties. I didn't have too much time to decide if I should go in one or not considering that the reason I was sick was because of the horrid smells.

I didn't have any more time to think as once again I knew my stomach was coming up. I rushed inside the furthest one the left and vomited roughly. I used a roll of toilet paper to wipe my mouth and thought it was kind of rude that the officer hadn't let me use a bathroom inside the Distribution Center.

As I was walking back towards the group, I picked up on what one of the policemen was explaining to Officer Grant.

"During the hurricane, a bunch of squatters broke into this building. They holed up inside taking refuge until just a few days ago; we found them and they were kicked out by the authorities. In the weeks that they were here, with the center having no working plumbing or toilets, they left their human excess in piles all throughout the building. There are human feces in every inch of that place and you can't get inside the building without protective gear on and a mask. It's impossible to even breathe." The policeman explained.

My steps had slowed as I overheard his words. My head tipped up and glanced at the building with widened eyes. All of the sudden the porter potty didn't seem so bad after all.

Officer Grant talked with the men for a few more moments while I stood there quietly taking down notes on my clipboard. As we were saying our goodbyes, I snapped a few quick photos before heading back to the car. As we drove further down the street, I kept my camera on to document the damage as we slowly drove by.

Here you could see the entire contents inside of these houses pulled out into the yards and sidewalks. Most of it was unsalvageable from the mold and water damage. The people just left it outside to be thrown away. You could still see dressers filled with clothes, file cabinets with important papers, boxes of toys and more. It was sad to see everything these people had owned left behind in an effort to survive themselves.

It was hard for me to imagine what the evacuees were feeling right now, knowing that I myself had never experienced losing everything that I had owned before. It really made me feel for them and at the same time, say a silent prayer of thanks for the blessings I had in my life. I wondered what people around the country were thinking when they thought of what Hurricane Katrina had done to the state.

I doubted that most could realize the extent of the damage as much as I could here by seeing it right in front of me. Being far away from home, away from the normal life everyone was still living back there, and seeing the horrific aftermath surrounding me, I felt like I was in a third-world country.

I just kept wondering how long it would take to really get this city back on its feet. The damage was so expansive, and the threat of contamination just from handling the belongings inside of the houses or really any of the buildings here was so significant. I truly had no idea how this city, in it's current condition could get back to some semblance of "normal" anytime in the new future. I really had to imagine it would take years.

The holes that you see in the top of this apartment building were punched out from rescuers attempting to get to the victims who were trapped inside from the rising waters. I cannot even begin to imagine how terrifying this would have been, to be trapped, threatening to drown, and not even being able to climb up on the roof. Thank goodness the rescuers were able to break through the roof to pull people out!

Massive fires raged after the storm, completely incinerating anything flammable. In this picture above, you can see that the only thing left standing in this fire was the doorframe. It was almost a strange, ironic taunt…"welcome to nothing".

Here is a closer view.

Here is a small rowboat left "docked" right in front of someone's front door. It was quite ironic to see this. As the waters had receded, and the flooding had dispersed, the rowboat was left on solid ground straight dab in the middle of the road.

The garbage and debris covered the ground like snow blanketing the grass in the winter months of the Northern states. *How do you even clean up all of this? Like how would you even begin?*

Spray-painted messages were everywhere. Some were warnings for people to stay out, including robbers, or just people in general, because the premises were full of contamination and would make them sick. Others contained symbols and X's that were coded to mark body counts (dead bodies found), pet counts and identify specific contamination threats.

It was typical to see the siding on the houses shredded from the fierceness of the hurricane's winds.

Abandoned parking lots were the perfect hot spots for car vandalism or theft. Many of them remained, with bashed out windows and the valuable items inside stolen. Even worse, most of the car dealerships had lost their entire inventory. Many of their cars had been vandalized too, many stolen, and the rest destroyed by the seawater's salty kiss.

    Brand new grocery stores stood vacant with the remains of what was left inside after having been broken into. The glass was completely shattered on the doors allowing the perfect entrance to rummage through and steal any thing inside, with no one to come after you.

    The police were too busy running around, scrambling to find any semblance of peace, and assisting the victims. It was very dangerous to be in any part of New Orleans at this point, and many of the people who were committing these crimes had weapons and were not afraid to use them.

    Whole towns quickly turned into ghost towns after the evacuation, which created the perfect opportunity for crime. It was a tragic distraction, which allowed criminals to pillage and plunder their way through the rubble, most of the time without consequence at this early stage of hurricane recovery.

Here is another shot of the grocery store. You can see the parking lot littered with debris and trash as well. *It was almost a scene out of a Zombie Apocalypse movie!* I was wondering how safe it was to be taking this photo in this moment. *Were there still criminals inside of the grocery store, or around the corner, or watching me watching their target of prey?*

I remember feeling bad for the owners too. How devastating to not only have a hurricane ruin your business, but then to have criminals, or even desperate victims stealing and vandalizing your business thereafter. Two vicious blows back to back. *I couldn't imagine!*

As night fell, Officer Grant and I pulled away from our last stop and headed back to Headquarters. I put my camera back in its case and my clipboard of notes in a satchel and leaned back in the seat to rest my eyes.

We had spent the entire day in meetings with the police and National Guard, scouting all of our Red Cross locations there, taking pictures of our findings and collecting data to take back to our department back in Baton Rouge. I was physically spent and once again eager to grab a few hours of sleep.

WEDNESDAY, OCTOBER 5th
STAFF SHELTERS
7:57 A.M.

Unbeknownst to me, today would be bringing me my biggest assignment yet. The long, trying, eye-opening experience of visiting New Orleans a day prior had left me thoroughly exhausted. I walked into Headquarters for the 8:00 meeting and to find out my next assignment.

Prior to my arrival, Officer Grant had already briefed the Lieutenant Colonel on the success of our reconnaissance in New Orleans. He'd even gone as far as to complement my assistance in navigating, photographing, communicating and gathering data in such a professional and competent manner. I was unaware of all this as I listened to the most recent updates of the operation and waited as assignments were passed out.

At the end of the meeting, I still hadn't received my assignment and stood back to let everyone get on with their duties. I was a little concerned at this point and then jumped a little bit, completely startled, when I heard the Lieutenant calling my name from where he stood over by his desk. *Oh no! This could only be bad news!*

For the life of me I was befuddled as to what trouble I could have gotten myself into this time and I prayed hurriedly that it was nothing too appalling.

"Rose," he said with a serious look on his face as I approached his desk. "Officer Grant has briefed me on your trip to New Orleans yesterday."

I nodded waiting for him to continue, eyes opened wide.

"I wanted to say that I'm so pleased with your work since you arrived here. Everything I have asked you to do, you have not only done, but you have done it competently and in a timely manner. You have many talents and you have attempted to use all of them to assist our department. You have foreign language skills in which you have used to communicate with every person that you have come into contact with whether or not they speak English. You are able to work in a professional manner, setting a precedent and an example to the others around you, despite their age." He paused.

"I am placing you in charge of all of the Staff Shelters."

"What do you mean?" I asked completely in shock.

"Well, I would like you to coordinate security measures and implement leadership roles in all of the shelters throughout Louisiana. But for now, you can start with Baton Rouge. We have 16 shelters here."

I nodded quickly quelling my surprise and accepted the challenge. I grabbed a notepad and pen to take down notes as the Lieutenant kept talking.

"What I would like you to do first is to develop a program that can be set up to carry our teams through the three-week department term. This program will teach our managers how to do their jobs, handle crises, and instruct the new managers on how to pick up where the old ones left off."

"Second, I want you to fire the guards that aren't doing their jobs, and hold the rest accountable to their duties. We have hired an outside security firm to guard our shelters and many have been slacking and sneaking off-site when they are supposed to be on duty. You will meet with the firm's head Security Officer to get the names and positions of all of the employees."

"Third, I want you to teach the managers how to effectively communicate with Safety and Security here at Headquarters. I want you to start having weekly meetings at all of the shelters to get updates on any occurrences and get copies of all incident reports."

"You will also start briefing us during our morning meetings here at Headquarters on your Staff Shelter Project. I will give you all the maps you need to find the shelters and the current manager's names so you can begin." He said finishing.

"So," I started, "Basically you want me to open a line of communication between our department and the Staff Shelters, find a way to create consistency, and tackle the current problems that exist within them."

"Exactly," he smiled. He knew I understood what he wanted and he also knew that I would be able to make it happen. This would certainly be my largest challenge yet. Just starting with 16 shelters in Baton Rouge would be a big feat. I was eager for the challenge and excited to prove to the Colonel that I could in fact do exactly what needed to be done.

I spent the next two days designing a program for all of the shelter managers. It was very lengthy and detailed and fit very nicely into individual binders. It included a training manual; the "do's and don'ts" while operating a shelter, the security requirements and procedures, and contact information.

The next three days I drove around Baton Rouge to hand deliver the program to all 16 managers. I spent a few moments introducing myself as the new Safety and Security liaison from Headquarters and getting to know all of the managers. Any needs, concerns or incidents were to be documented from this point out, delivered to me and taken back to the Department. I would spend the majority of my remaining time in Louisiana doing this job.

Here I am carrying my knife, cell phone, SAS phone, walkie-talkie, binder, clipboards, keys, sunglasses and most importantly coffee! <smile> My daily load of stuff needed just to coordinate all of the Staff Shelters.

THURSDAY, OCTOBER 6th
SENDING WORD BACK HOME
3:20 A.M.

It was in the wee hours of the morning and I still had not left Headquarters yet. Mere hours from now I would be asked to report back to the same place for my 8:00 a.m. briefing. My eyes drooped heavily and my limbs hung weakly as my fingers pressed tiredly on the computer keys. I needed rest and I needed it desperately, but I couldn't stop until I had sent a short message home with the latest updates of my deployment.

I felt that by informing those back in Michigan of my circumstances, they would have a better understanding of how things were down here and perhaps could find a way of their own to help. The only time I had to write home would be when I was sent off duty, and that was usually after one or two a.m.

A typical shift was between 12 and 18 hours a day for anyone who worked out of Headquarters. I was telling myself that sleep was a luxury on this trip and by no means a necessity.

The deployment was a three-week assignment and I felt that every waking moment was a moment I needed to be working. That was why I had come to Louisiana and if it meant that I had to sacrifice my beauty sleep, then by far it was a sacrifice that I was willing to make. This tour wasn't about me and I wanted to make each moment count. I had plenty of time left in my lifetime to take a vacation or relax.

On this particular evening, my eyes nearly closed as I typed. The security guards kept walking by to make sure everything was okay and kept asking when my "book" was going to be done. I was the only volunteer left in the building save for the guards and it was sort of strange to see such a young girl so intent on typing this late at night.

The guards knew from the prior nights I had sat at the same computer typing that sometimes I could sit there working on an email for several hours before finally leaving the building to go catch two or three hours of sleep. In a sense, the presence of the guards and their warm support inspired me, and it was in these early hours that I had no distractions in my mind and could just release the events of the day.

The following email is the introduction to the letter that I sent home on October 6th, 2005.

EMAIL COORESPONDENCE
4:58 A.M.

Dear All,

Is seems like forever since I wrote last. Working in crisis management truly makes one feel like the day never begins nor ends. The drama here comes in the form of one crisis after the next. Our department is working diligently to try to maintain some sort of order here.

In reference to the 9th Ward section of New Orleans for those of you who are unaware, I want you to know if it's danger. The 9th Ward has always been an unsafe place to live, but after the hurricane it has become an even more volatile place.

Prior to the storm, the 9th Ward was known as a very poor area with residents who had no definable income. It is safe to say that a lot of residents found other ways to survive even if it meant having to use a gun or knife. Having this in mind, with the onslaught of Hurricane Katrina, the 9th Ward as well as many others with similar lifestyles were unleashed here in Baton Rouge.

The now homeless residents are seeking refuge in a city that now has a surplus of over 100,000 extra bodies. The problems that Louisiana had before the storm did not disappear after its retreat. In all honesty, they worsened to the point where Louisiana now reminds me of a third-world country. The crime is rampant and the authorities are grasping at straws to maintain order.

The safe, secure and stable system, in which Louisiana had been struggling to maintain before, is now on the verge of collapse. It is complete madness and it is out of control. As sad as it is to say, the arrival of the hurricane left the perfect guise for dishonest people to hide under, a perfect cloak to cover their crime.

Howell Park, the shelter that I had stayed in my first night in Baton Rouge had another shooting incident just a week after the one I had experienced. Big surprise, eh! It didn't take but a quick thought to close down the shelter and relocate it.

Howell Park is located in a very dangerous part of town, and I still wonder how it was ever opened in the first place. Needless to say, nobody was hurt there that was volunteering on the Operation, and that has to count for something.

In the midst of a meeting I was having with the Lieutenant, a bulky man supporting a distraught, tear-stained woman interrupted us. We were told that the woman had just been a victim of an assault.

The Lieutenant stood up just then and whispered in my ear, "I think she needs the Rosie touch." I swallowed quickly refraining from letting my jaw drop at his quick departure. He left me standing there to handle the situation alone.

I was a little taken off guard and didn't understand why I was the one to deal with an assault victim rather than a police officer. I put on a smile and tried to be strong for the woman, understanding what it must be like to be in her shoes.

I figured two weak people couldn't solve anything and that I had to act strong and confident if I was going to be able to help her. It is an unspoken responsibility of an authoritative figure to use sensibility and strength to overcome problems and leave out the rollercoaster of emotions.

I was just a young girl here, not authoritative in any way. But at the same time, people here were losing it left and right and no matter what, I figured someone had to keep their head on their shoulders.

I briefly took the woman's hands into my own and kindly asked her to explain what had happened. My heart broke as I watched the tears slip down her face and I patiently waited until I had gotten enough information to file an incident report to hand over to the police.

I handed her a few tissues and asked if I could take her to the Oasis to get a snack and some water. I saw a little glimmer of hope then as she followed me there. I don't think she wanted to be alone and it seemed that she found comfort being around another woman who she knew was trying to help her.

En route to Baton Rouge on an afternoon return trip from New Orleans we happened upon one of the most gut-wrenching sights I have seen yet. Up ahead on the highway, pulled off to the side of the road, was a battered vehicle with smoke pouring out of the hood.

An elderly man lay hunched over the wheel gasping in hyperventilating spurts of air. If the tanned wrinkles covering his face weren't a sign of his age, the white tufts of hair sticking up haphazardly all around his face sure were.

The man had to be in his eighties. Sweat poured down his aged face in the ninety-degree heat, and his lungs struggled to catch air. An oxygen tube ran under his nose running all the way down into a tank that was lying next to him. His eyes lay closed using every effort possible to breathe.

It was a cheap little car, and according to the looks of things, it contained every possession the man possibly owned, completely packed to the brim. The elderly man was coming out of New

Orleans, with his car holding everything valuable to him, to seek a future somewhere out West.

The man had no water with him, no food and really no way to survive, let alone make it out of his car trouble situation. He was pretty much left for dead and as I tell the story, I am reminded of the Good Samaritan.

The Good Samaritan is a story from the Bible where a man had been beaten and tossed on the roadside, left to die, and only one man was kind enough to stop and help him. Here we were on the road back to Baton Rouge, and had stumbled upon a man left to die on the side of this road.

To make matters worse, there were no working gas stations, repair shops, or any shops of any sorts that were open after the hurricane in this area. All of the gas had been contaminated in the New Orleans area, the electric lines destroyed and buildings damaged and flooded. There was no help around. It was a sober reminder that "we were the help here"...if you got into trouble you were on your own.

The outer edges of the city were now abandoned. The police and authorities were elsewhere fighting to maintain order in the locations where there were actually people around. It was desolate, deserted and a disaster waiting to happen for anyone that ran into trouble coming out of New Orleans.

Not only were there no tow trucks to take this man to get his car fixed, there were no ambulances to take him to the hospital before he suffered a tragic death from heatstroke. In essence, it would be up to us, the Red Cross, to save this man's life, and we did.

I am feasting on MRE's and packaged meals. They're not too bad, but still pale in comparison to a hearty, home-cooked meal. They are high in calories, but I still never feel full after eating one. Since I am out in the field almost every day and have precious little time to even eat a meal I am surviving on these.

It is one of the things I dream about most here...having a nice steak dinner with fries and chocolate milk when I return to Michigan! Oh! And ketchup too! ☺ Mmm...and can't forget pickles!

    I will keep sending little updates home to you guys, as I am able. Hope all is going well up there and thank you so much for all of your prayers.

Somewhere out there,

Rosie the Riveter

Sending home little messages always made me feel like I still had a connection with my life back there. Waking up every day on a relief operation, full of constant crises, made it easy to forget sometimes what a normal life used to be like.

Down here, I never had a spare moment to think. My time was spent wrapped up in a whole different world of devastation and destruction. It almost seemed to become part of my daily life.

My family, my friends, my bills, my home, everything came to be a far away memory. I didn't really feel a sense of homesickness, but rather a sense of loneliness. A loneliness that was hidden by the smile I gave in an attempt to be strong for those that needed strength. And that was what gave me the courage every day to get up and do it all over again. To know that if I could make someone else smile, my time here would be worth it.

FRIDAY, OCTOBER 7th
STAKEOUT
2:45 P.M.

It was a blistery, hot afternoon, a deceitful retreat of stormy weather and an introduction of warm, sunny coziness. It was hard to believe that just several weeks prior, a mad storm had ravaged this part of the country. It would appear that nature was toying with random possibilities and perchance couldn't make up its mind as to which temperament to flaunt.

I was sitting at a desk at the State and Security department just finishing up filing an incident report, when Officer Grant came over with a big smile on his face.

"Rose, what are you up to?" He asked.

I paused for a moment slipping the folder back in place as I thought, *what is he up to?* Officer Grant was a comical character, always wearing a huge smile, always diplomatic, fair and upstanding in his decisions. I respected him a lot.

"Hmm...should I take a guess or just brace myself for what you are going to say next?" I teased lightly.

Grant's smile widened.

"I think I have something you might be interested in helping out with. He said, cocking his head slightly to the left in an amusing gesture. Officer Grant was always using his hands, his arms or anything else to exemplify the words of his conversation, turning it into more of a theatrical play than a simple dialogue.

"You've got my attention," I said with a slow grin.

"First, are you busy?" Grant questioned his chin dropping slightly, bringing his face closer to my eye level as if to say "I don't want to intrude". Grant was very polite and no matter how important the situation was, he always approached it in a non-invasive way.

"No, actually I was just finishing up this incident report. I'm done for the moment." I replied as I gave him my full, undivided attention, folding my arms casually on the desktop waiting for whatever was to come.

"Ok, here's the deal. Perimeter security just informed us of a situation outside of the building. You have to keep very quiet about this because we don't know how serious it is.

"Sure," I murmured quietly.

"There is a man just outside the Headquarters facility, around the left side of the building, that is handing out forms to get Red Cross debit cards."

"But we don't assist clients here at Headquarters." I interrupted in question. ("Clients" was the term we used for the hurricane victims.)

"I know. That's the problem." Grant continued. "He isn't allowed to be assisting clients here, so he's probably running an illegitimate operation."

"What do you mean exactly?" I said raising one eyebrow.

"Well, for one, the man is all by himself. Two, he is requesting personal financial information from hurricane victims. Three, for all we know, he could be operating a money scam right under our noses, using the Red Cross as a cover."

"Hmm…" I said pondering for a moment. "Who is he and where is he from?" I finally finished with a slight shake of the head.

"Well that is the strangest part. He is claiming to be from the Red Cross!"

I let out a deep sigh. *The drama never ended did it?*

"Sure, I'm in," I began in a serious tone. "What do you need me to do?"

"Well, this is the best part of all and I know you are going to love it!" Grant said eagerly. "I want you to come on a stakeout with me to observe the situation outside and to see if Safety and Security needs to step in. We are responsible for any fraudulent activities, so we are required to look into it."

"Stakeout!" I repeated his words with a strange smile. I immediately thought of the movie "*I Spy*" where actor Owen Wilson plays a special agent. He dreams of the day, any day, or everyday really that he would be able to do a stakeout.

Every time someone says "stakeout", Owen Wilson repeats the word and jumps up and down like he's just received a million dollars. For some reason, he finds it to be such a thrilling spy technique, and it captivates him so much that he uses the word 'stakeout' in every other line of his conversation.

Bringing myself back to the situation at hand I nodded at Grant saying, "I'm ready!" *This should be interesting.* I never once envisioned myself being asked to do a stakeout when I had volunteered to come down here. In all reality, I didn't see myself doing half of the things I had already done on the Operation and tried to convince myself that perhaps this was just normal.

"We don't have a lot of time so we're just going to have to wing it."

"Alright," I said. I figured that was probably best in this situation anyways. At least we would be more natural in responding to whatever was about to happen.

"We'll take my Jeep and drive around to a spot in the parking lot that is out of the man's view but close enough to where we can still watch and observe him." Grant quickly added.

I followed him out of Headquarters swallowing dryly as a thick wave of blazing heat hit my face. By the time we reached his vehicle, sweat was trickling down my skin over much of my body. As much as this would have bothered me on a normal day, causing me to either jump in the water or go inside where there was air conditioning, I found that on the operation it didn't bother me as much.

It is hard to explain, but it was easy to lose sight of yourself here when so many others needed your help. I didn't have to look good or dress nice. I didn't have to get my beauty rest, wear nice-smelling perfume, blow-dry my hair or wear fancy jewelry.

I was just a normal soul here with only my hands and my heart to work with. It sounds crazy but it was so amazing to me. The world we live in is run on a timed clock. From the moment we are born, we are placed into a race. This race is the push to grow up, to make money, to get a house, have a nice car and to go somewhere in life and to be someone important.

At the checkpoints in the race, one pauses to make sure their tie is secured just right, suit coat fit snugly, one's makeup doesn't need a touchup, one's dress and jewelry will stand out from all the other women, the cash in one's wallet is enough to last through the week and that one's credit card has a high enough limit to book the next vacation.

I was starting to realize that this race we all enter is only pushing us to the finish faster. That finish being the end of our lives, and the day we are placed into the grave.

The luxuries in life seem to be the most sought after thing. It is a pull that keeps everyone pushing with the ones left behind struggling to catch up.

Coming to Louisiana, and being snatched out of that race in a sense really made me see a new view from the outside looking in.

It was the first time in my life that I didn't feel pressured to be someone or to have to look good. Perhaps this is what made me fit right in down here, while most struggled to keep up with the crisis management and the changes.

Most people didn't even know how to handle not having a bed to sleep in, a warm shower every night, a home-cooked dinner, a nice vehicle to drive around in, an X-box to play, movies to watch, books to read, or some a beer to drink while they sit in front of the T.V.

We are so used to having everything we need but constantly running in this race because it is never enough and we always want more. It is this unhappy state that will always keep us running, and never stopping long enough to appreciate what we have, or ever realize that this is all we will ever need.

<u>I started to realize that this race made one starve with a hunger that would never be sated</u>. When we take our last breath, all that remains is our character. The only thing that truly matters is who we are, (or were), not what we have. It is our heart, our love and what we have to give to someone else that matters most. That is our legacy.

Without people, family, friends and that special someone, our lives are empty of meaning and purpose. They say that the only love one has is the love they give. We choose to give or to take. But at the end of our journey, it is what we gave that is remembered, not the things we attained.

    I felt a strange sense of peace in the midst of constant crisis happening all around me. I felt like all I had to give here, or could give, was just myself; every talent I possessed: my heart, my smile and that special something within that sparked a smile in others. My efforts were inspiring them and giving them hope that things would get better for them soon.

    I felt as if I was giving my all, something that didn't cost a penny and it was all that was needed to make a difference. It was starting to be the greatest accomplishment I had ever achieved. I was finally starting to see what it felt like to think of someone else and to leave all selfish acts for one's own glory left behind in another time and place.

    To know that I didn't have to try to be something or someone important…no, just me as is…was enough. It was all that was needed here and it was making all the difference to someone.

    I didn't think about the race anymore. I didn't think about all the pressure that came with running in it or trying to keep up with those that were so much further ahead of me.

    I was wearing the simplest, almost unattractive clothing, hair that hung wildly around my shoulders, tennis shoes even. I have never worn tennis shoes in my entire life! It was amazing knowing that I was a real person here with something real to give. If only we could all one day just put down the façade and the face we put on to try to be something, perhaps then, we would realize that who we are inside is enough to be happy every day we are alive.

As we climbed into the vehicle I glanced quickly at Grant as he slowly turned down the volume on the radio. It was as if an unsaid message passed between us as he caught my eyes. I felt a deep sense of confidence and respect from him being directed towards me, and it gave me such a greater desire to do a good job.

I remained silent as Grant pulled the car around trying to covertly look for the perfect stakeout position. I pulled my sunglasses on and let the soft tones of the music playing calm the level of apprehension.

I glanced at the dull, gray façade of the building trying to pinpoint where the man in question was. Up and over to my left I noticed him, a medium-height guy with dark black hair standing over a small square brown table. His head was bent as he talked with a small group of pedestrians. On the table lay several stacks of paper contrasting white against the red color of his Red Cross uniformed shirt.

"There he is," I murmured softly to Grant.

Grant glanced over to where I held my gaze and nodded pulling into a parking spot between a large white van and a small pickup truck. From our location we had the perfect vantage point, and with the bright sunlight of the day, a strong glare would hit the vehicle's windows making it difficult to see inside the shadowy recesses.

Grant put the car into park and turned the air conditioning on. We both turned then to watch and wait. It is always best to observe a situation before jumping in. Often times, prior conceptions can easily become post-misconceptions resulting in unexpected surprises. At least here, we could see what we'd be up against should we have to step in.

We sat there and observed the man calling out to random passersby to stop at his table, listen to his speech and then proceed to fill out some sort of paperwork. This same scenario kept repeating itself. After twenty minutes or so had passed, I started to feel like we weren't accomplishing enough.

"Officer Grant, I think we need to get closer." I began. "I don't think we are going to learn any more sitting here watching. The man appears to be alone like you said earlier, but we need to find out what he's saying to everyone and what type of paperwork he's handing out."

"You're right," Grant agreed turning to glance at me.

"Why don't you let me pretend to be one of those pedestrians and see if he tries to stop me and persuade me to come over to his table. Then I can try to find out what is actually going on." I asked on a whim.

Because Officer Grant didn't want our department to be responsible for causing a scene, he'd opted to do a stakeout first. I understood that, but it still wasn't solving the problem that this guy might be committing fraud and possibly stealing people's identities. I didn't want to lose the opportunity to stop someone from doing something criminal, especially since it was happening right in front of our eyes.

To my utter shock and surprise, Officer Grant approved my offer.

"I have a feeling you already know what to do my Little Spy," he replied smiling. I thought it funny he said that because Grant knew just six months prior I had been offered my dream job to be a spy with the

NSA (The National Security Agency), and that shortly afterwards, I had turned it down! But that is another story for another time.

"I truly think you'll accomplish the job better than I could because of your youthful age and non-imposing attitude. I think the man might question me or get suspicious if I go!" Grant finished.

I just shook my head smirking a little as I eagerly unsnapped my seatbelt and sat up straight. My movements were deft and quick. I didn't want to lose our chance here. My thoughts were going a million miles a minute and my body parts were fumbling just trying to keep up.

I quickly tore off my Red Cross badge. By no means could I be caught in affiliation with the Red Cross when I was trying to assume the role of a hurricane victim. I would never find out any information then and would only cause the man to flee if our assumptions were right.

I then pulled the knife off my belt and set it next to my discarded badge in the Jeep's center console. I reached down and took off my black belt and unbuttoned my white dress shirt, taking it off while leaving my white t-shirt on underneath.

In addition, I took off my work cell phone and walkie-talkie laying them next to the other belongings. I pulled my hair into a ponytail and adjusted my brown tortoise-shell sunglasses without a mirror. I turned to see Grant watching me with a huge grin on his face.

"You are something else," he said shaking his head.

"I think this is the quickest I can change from a professional Safety and Security position to the "role" of a hurricane victim." I said laughing. I was doubtful that the man had a weapon, but I didn't have too much time to think about it with the new wave of adrenaline that I felt.

"Oops, I forgot my ring and my watch." I said as I dropped them quickly into the console. I wanted to look as casual and comfortable as possible. I decided to keep my personal cell phone on me just in case I had to contact Officer Grant. I did take off the phone clip though, so I could hide the phone in my hand.

"Well, this is it. I'm gonna head over there, check things out, just ask a few questions and try to get a copy of the paperwork. Once I get the papers, I will come straight back here, ok?"

"Alrighty, I'll have my eye on you the whole time so if you need anything, I've got your back." Officer Grant replied slipping his sunglasses on.

I nodded quickly and turned to open the door. I flipped open my cell phone as if just receiving a call and shut the Jeep door. I began to walk nonchalantly over towards where the man stood. I mumbled a few words into my cell phone to the imaginary person who had just "called".

I nodded my head in slight exasperation as I strode up to the desk. The corner of the building from where the man stood jutted right into an adjoining store. It was some sort of grocery mart, and I was pleased to have found the perfect exit strategy.

I quickly snapped my cell phone shut several feet from the booth and tried to act as if I was just going to pass the man by. Just as I anticipated from my prior surveillance, the man called out to me.

"Miss, could I talk to you for a moment?"

I hesitated slightly, somewhat uneasy when I noticed then that I was the only person there.

"Sure, I said calmly, taking a deep breath and headed slowly over to his table. As I got closer, I noticed him looking around fervently as if he was waiting for someone. He seemed a little uneasy and it made me all the more suspicious.

"Have you been affected by Hurricane Katrina and are you currently in need of financial assistance from the Red Cross?"

I paused for a moment looking him straight in the eyes. I realized that by answering, I would be solely on his turf and completely at the mercy of my ability to keep up the charade.

"Yes, I have been affected." I replied softly pulling a strand of hair out of my face.

"Where were you living when Katrina hit?" He asked next.

"In New Orleans," I said quickly thinking that he couldn't question that location. I wondered where he was going with this. He hadn't even introduced himself or explained why he was asking such personal questions. The man's next question made my heart stop for a moment wondering how I was going to keep my cover.

"What zip code exactly?" The man asked.

My heart was pounding in my chest. I hated to lie. I just never could do it. It was so deceitful and I could never understand how one ever got away with doing it. To lie is to pretend to be something you're not and it's cowardly, never being able to admit the real truth.

I didn't want to lie. I just needed more time to think! What zip code? Hmm...I had no clue. *"Well sir, actually I'm all the way from Michigan, I actually don't know one single zip code from Louisiana, let alone the one from New Orleans where I'm supposed to be from..."*

I smiled weakly at the man stealing a few more seconds to come up with a reasonable explanation for why I couldn't remember my own zip code.

"Actually," I said looking him in the eyes once again, putting on a bold front and an act of defensiveness. "Before I give out my personal information, I am more curious to see what sort of assistance the Red Cross can give to me. I don't mean to be rude, but I'm just not one of those people that jumps into things." I didn't pause in my explanation. "Is there any way I could take one of those forms with me, look it over, and then get back to you on it?" I finished with an innocent smile.

Secretly, my heart was still pounding rapidly, as I waited to see if my strategy would work. I didn't know if the man would buy my story and from the strange look on his face, I could see he was a little miffed.

In all reality, I don't know one single person in Louisiana affected by Hurricane Katrina that would not have jumped at any opportunity for financial assistance. I was hoping that he wouldn't realize this fast enough and that his irritated look wasn't enough to lose my chance to get ahold of the papers.

"Oh, and I assume you'll be back here later on right?" I continued thinking fast. I said this to try to reassure him that I was coming back, but also so I could find out how much time we would have to investigate my findings before he had time to disappear.

"Yeah, I'll be here," the man said not too assuredly. I didn't like the sound of that.

I could tell he was slightly taken aback by my response. He finally nodded his head in agreement, handed me a form with a frown and stood back. I slowly took the form, peeked at it for a few seconds as if perusing its contents and then turned to walk away.

"I have to run into the store now but thank you for the form. I'll look it over and come back." I said with a wave.

I swallowed feeling a huge lump in my throat and escaped quickly into the grocery store a few feet from where I'd been standing. I ignored the stares of the rest of the new bystanders approaching and welcomed the huge wave of cool air that hugged me as the store door closed behind me.

Wow! I had gotten away with it! I had walked away with proof...the paperwork that I clutched in my left hand! It was at that moment I realized that I had no cash on me to buy anything inside of the store. *Oh no! The man was going to think I was lying about having to come in here!* He would totally see me when I walked out, even if I went out the other sliding door away from the one I had just entered.

Thinking quickly, holding my cell phone and the paperwork in my hand, I walked up to one of the cashiers who didn't have any customers and asked for a plastic bag.

Hoping the woman didn't think I was asking for one to go steal stuff, I waited patiently and breathed a sigh of relief when she casually handed me one. I mumbled a quick thanks and walked over to a large bulletin board that had a bunch of ads hanging up so that I could kill a few more seconds "shopping".

After I felt a reasonable enough time had passed, I stuck my phone and the papers in the plastic bag and walked calmly out of the store. I ignored the man and his table and headed back towards where Officer Grant had parked the Jeep. I quickly climbed in and filled him in on all the details. He asked to look at the paperwork and as I was handing it to him, my work cell phone rang, still lying next to my other belongings in the Jeep's console.

Grant took the papers and I answered my cell phone. It was the Lieutenant Colonel who said that he had an emergency situation in the Mental Health Department and he needed me to immediately go escort someone out of the building. I quickly informed Grant of the situation and left him alone to handle the rest of the stakeout.

Later on, I found out that we had been too late. Officer Grant had went in to show the paperwork to the Financial Department inside Headquarters, and by the time they went back outside, the man had vanished and was missing. We also found out that his paperwork really had been a ruse to get people's financial information! *Well, at least we had been able to make him nervous enough to stop his plot at Headquarters! At least we'd done that!*

SATURDAY, OCTOBER 8th
STRANDED
7:00 P.M.

On my third trip into New Orleans, I encountered my first real-life experience of what it would be like to be in a horror movie. One person's carelessness, just a simple mistake, would turn into the hardest trial and scariest of moments.

It was a night trip where I was asked to ride along as a guide through the routes I had just been on with Officer Grant several days prior. Because there weren't any road signs left in the city, it was literally impossible to navigate through New Orleans without a personal guide. I was accompanying two technicians and a computer analyst.

In the front seat was Frank our driver, in the passenger seat was Brent the computer analyst and Nina the other technician was sitting next to me in the back seat. This was the first time that I had met any of the three passengers in the vehicle with me.

I had been asked to go along as a guide to help these three workers become familiar with the routes in New Orleans, since I had been one of the first members from Headquarters to re-enter the city after they had recently re-opened it.

We left Headquarters around 7:00 p.m. in the evening after our daily assignments had been completed. I was used to not sleeping and adjusted to the fact that even after my necessary duties had been completed, sleep was still a luxury.

There were always other tasks, obligations, or responsibilities on a massive relief operation such as this. Your 24-hour day turned into a simple three-week block, and the hours turned into days, days turned into weeks and weeks turned into your deployment term. In essence, this meant that your meals and sleep never came on a schedule. They came perchance if you were lucky.

Unbeknownst to us, as our vehicle pulled away from Headquarters in Baton Rouge and headed towards I-10, we were leaving behind our only opportunity to fill up on gas. Even worse, we were unaware that the tank was already on E.

I was in the backseat, so there was no way I could have known about our current, escalating dilemma. On top of it, this was only my third venture into New Orleans, and I was still learning myself of the risk factors.

No matter what, it was the driver's responsibility to check the gas gauge, not the passengers, and he failed to do that. So as we headed into the black night towards the city of doom, all four of us volunteers carried on casual conversation in attempt to break the ice, completely unaware that our vehicle was losing its precious last drops of gas.

I sat in the backseat trying to learn a little bit about my fellow passengers. Brent, the guy in the front seat, was a shy young man who didn't speak unless spoken to. He was friendly nonetheless, but felt more comfortable to listen than to converse.

The lady sitting to my right in the backseat was the talker of the bunch, and I found very quickly that I began to get annoyed. She was the type of person that had a hard time with absolute silence and would rather hear her own voice than no voice at all.

And of course, our driver was focused on the road, but I could gather from his little chatter here and there that he was a personable guy and a pretty laid-back individual.

I began tooning out the lady sitting next to me, annoyed with her babble, and peered into the thick blackness outside my window. It was a spooky night, devoid of any visible moon or sparkling stars.

There were random haggard splotches off to the sides of the roadway that could be pieced into the shapes of trees. The only light came from the lights of the few cars driving on highway.

We seemed to be the only vehicle heading into New Orleans at this specific time of night. They had a curfew in the city and it was better to get things done in the daytime.

The repartee going on back and forth between the others slowly dwindled to a dim muffled sound in my head. The mood was extremely carefree, and bouts of laughter kept the banter going. I found myself letting a small smile escape my lips at humor of the circumstance.

My thoughts drifted ironically towards home, my home in Michigan. A sort of sadness hit me just then. I felt displaced in a way, distant from the life everyone still lived back there. I always felt that way when I traveled. I wasn't homesick, but I missed those I loved. I always felt bad leaving them behind at the expense of pursuing my own destiny.

Traveling the world was a strong passion of mine. It was close to my heart, necessary for my work, and required for the experience I needed to do my job. It made me appreciate the small things in life, and made the bigger ones seems so much less attractive. I felt a strong purpose in my life to make each moment, each day count.

I wanted more than anything to change the world in some way. It was all part of my daily pursuit. I wanted to live a life that inspired others. Someone once said, "I'm planting a seed for a tree today, so that seven years later someone else can enjoy the shade." When I die, I want people to be able to look back and say...yes, Rose made a difference.

The sudden slam of the brakes and the whiplash from the abrupt reduction in speed caused me to immediately come out of my reverie.

I quickly peered ahead into the blackness noticing huge construction signs blocking off the highway up ahead. A strong barricade of orange, black and white meshed into a thick mirage of colors blinding our view and blocking our passage.

What had happened was not quite clear, except for the fact that we would have to exit the highway and take the back roads into New Orleans. *Great!* This was only my third tour to New Orleans and already the routes were foiled. *I wouldn't be much help now.*

We were forced to exit the highway and find a new route. To make matters worse, it was pitch black and there was no moon. It was then that a bad situation began to get worse. The moment our vehicle veered off the highway and turned right onto a random street, the lights of the town behind us begin to slip further and further away.

At this point, Frank was just driving on a whim trying to find a road parallel to the highway and follow that into New Orleans. Nina's demeanor changed and she started going off like a windup doll that would not stop chanting. She started to get scared and kept talking just to keep sound in the vehicle. Her fear played through her words, and her frantic gestures caused the tension to rise in the car.

I clamped my mouth shut, desperately holding in the urge to turn and tell her to just be quiet. Brent was completely silent upfront and Frank was mumbling to himself as he tried to steer the vehicle around abandoned construction rubble.

It seemed like the beginnings of a bad scene that could only get worse. Something just didn't feel right. It was a feeling of foreboding…a feeling that something bad was in the works and that we were all of the sudden the only actors in this play.

I could see the three people in the car with me off in their own little worlds. It was as if a sheet of ice had slipped in through the windows and placed each person inside a sculpture of fear.

Nina was frantically babbling about which way Frank should take and begging him to turn around and try to find the lights of the last town we'd passed through. Brent turned to face me and gave me a silent stare of, *"Why do I feel like we are the only two sensible ones here?"* I couldn't stand the suspense any longer.

"Frank, do you have a map?" I asked sternly, leaning forward and catching his attention.

"Yes, I think so, in the trunk." He replied thinly.

"Pull over." I said firmly.

Frank didn't argue. He glanced up briefly in the rear-view mirror, caught my unwavering gaze and quickly pulled the car over onto the shoulder causing a small poof of dust to swirl upwards, which quickly disappeared into the pool of darkness.

There was a pregnant pause as Frank put the car into park. Nobody moved for a moment. It seemed as if dark shadows started dancing towards our lone car and as if the blackness of night started to seep in through the cracks, threatening to drown us in its muse.

Not a sound was heard outside, and it seemed as if something was calmly waiting for one of us to open the door before snatching us up into the night. There were no shapes visible, no life, no buildings…nothing outside our vehicle. There was just lonely, dry grass and a street lamp with no light bulb.

I reached with my right hand to touch my hip feeling for my knife. *It wasn't there! Oh no!*

"Does anyone have a weapon?" I asked quickly.

Everyone just turned and stared at me…their silence was answer enough. *That would be a negative.*

Why had I not brought my knife? How could I have been so careless? We were completely defenseless, all alone, and stranded in the middle of nowhere. There were no cops, no citizens, no military…nothing.

The only people that would be here right now would be the very criminals that were looting and creating unlawful havoc on the less unfortunate after the hurricane.

It was safe to say that you didn't even trust the cops. You didn't trust anyone. It was a desolate part of Louisiana, completely abandoned and off the map. We weren't safe here and we needed to move fast.

The sharp rasp of my door opening made everyone jump.

"Frank, come with me." I said loudly.

He glanced up sharply and quickly turned and warily got out of the car. Before closing my door, I leaned in and told Brent to pop the trunk. If our vehicle with its two piercing headlights pouring out front into an eerie black night wasn't obvious enough of our presence, the loud slam of car doors surely had awakened even the most unaware mortal.

I quickly went around to the back of the vehicle feeling the hairs on the back of my neck and arms stiffen as I felt the night closing in on us. I felt completely vulnerable to attack and even more, completely defenseless to prevent it.

"Frank, you have to find the map." I said opening the lid of the trunk. "Do you have a flashlight?" I asked opening my cell phone, using the meager light to try to locate the map.

"No," Frank said licking his lips nervously.

"Here it is," I murmured grabbing a map hiding under a thin blue sweatshirt. "Get back in the car," I said slamming the trunk closed.

We both climbed back into the vehicle closing the doors simultaneously. Brent quickly pushed the lock button securing the vehicle as best as was possible. I flipped my cell phone over looking at the bars on top trying to gauge how much service we had in this desolate area and felt a skip in the beating of my heart as I noticed the "no service" symbol in the left-hand corner. I swallowed quickly.

"We have to hurry," I said. "It isn't safe to just rest here. We are sitting ducks. Frank, you have to locate us on the map."

I held my cell phone over the tangled web of roads and junctions. It dimly lit up so that Frank could locate us and try to find the quickest way back to life, existence, and lights.

I kept peering outside checking for changes in our surroundings, new shadows that perhaps were moving, and listened for sounds…anything that would hint at a presence other than the four of us in our lone vehicle.

"Well it looks like the road we are currently on is Jefferson Avenue and if we continue straight on it, it will eventually take us directly into New Orleans." Frank said matter-of-factly.

Great! I thought. We either keep heading into the dark lonely, empty ghost towns of Louisiana on a hope that we'll run into our destination city or we turn around and try to find our way back to the highway and to the lights of the last town that we saw. It was the perfect "Choose Your Own Adventure Story" except this wasn't a story this was a "Real-Life Adventure".

"Alright, let's go." I said pointing further down Jefferson Avenue. "This is our best option. It is dangerous, but if we keep moving and don't stop, we will get into New Orleans faster than if we would turn around and try to find our way back to the highway." I took a deep breath.

"We may just end up even more turned around and who knows where we could end up. I don't want to have to paint those scenarios." I paused for a moment letting my words sink in. "We have to move."

"I think she's right," Brent said quietly.

"Yeah, but I don't think we should keep going further down this road. Who knows what is out there and the further we go, the farther we get away from people, from help. We have to turn around." Nina quickly babbled her voice taking on a high-whining pitch. *Yea,h well we are the help Nina…we are the help, there is no one to help us right now,* I thought dryly.

"We have to keep going, it's our strongest option," Frank finally said. "Keep your eyes peeled," he continued and quickly pulled the car back on the road.

And that was that. We continued on our way down the lonely, deserted avenue with each second taking us further and further from whence we came, and closer and closer to whatever lay ahead. Whatever that was, we would surely find out.

The sudden "ding, ding, ding" sound of the "low fuel alert" caused everyone to jump inside the car. Nobody moved. Nobody said anything. The fear was so thick in the car that we all just gripped the sides of the doors, hanging on as if it would keep this horrible tragic event from spinning any further out of control. We were out of gas and driving on fumes.

I bowed my head and I prayed. I asked God to protect us, to be the guide of our vehicle, and to have His angels watch over us. I prayed for a miracle, and asked Him to allow our car to continue to drive, even with no more gas, until we were safely back to civilization. I opened my eyes, and looked up ahead at the dark, gloomy road, and believed, that by faith, God would answer my prayer.

Ten minutes later, we were still driving…driving down Jefferson Avenue, when we ran smack dab into a military checkpoint. They were so shocked to see us in such a dangerous area and said that we were lucky to be alive. They were able to help us re-fuel our car and escort us safely into New Orleans. It was nothing short of a miracle. *Thank you God! Thank you for answering my prayer.*

SUNDAY, OCTOBER 8th
UPDATE
3:03 P.M.

Basically ever since I was placed in charge of all the Staff Shelters, I became my own boss. Now I brief the head of Safety and Security, and in the midst of all the fieldwork, inspections and trips, I am having meetings with SAS, Staff Services, the Security Firm, and the police throughout Louisiana.

Several of the latest incidents are as follows: one, meeting with the Baton Rouge Police Department concerning a larceny at one of my shelters, two, deflecting the media at another, and three, investigating with the Sheriff as to how someone had gotten pinned up against a metal door by being electrocuted! That incident was at the Lamar-Dixon client shelter, which has since been placed under my supervision with Safety and Security.

Earlier this week the National Guard snuck an entire case of MRE's in the back seat of my car because they said I was wasting away, and knew how happy I was to eat MRE's in general, as most people hate them.

How sweet of them! They also made sure to mention, along with the Sheriff's Department, that I am not allowed to leave Louisiana until I go back to the compound to give a formal goodbye. So today, I tracked down a case of Oreo cookies, which I plan to hand out as my goodbye gift to them on the Wednesday before I leave.

In the evenings, in between changing from day shift to night routine, I've been trying to play the piano in the shelters for the hour that dinner is being served.

It is amazing just what music can do to calm one's mood and alleviate tensions. Music is healing, therapeutic really, and can so quickly soothe the soul. It is the one thing that can unite everyone together in a single moment, no matter what life they come from.

SUNDAY, OCTOBER 9th
The Assault (#1)
7:39 P.M.

Walking down the cobblestone sidewalks of Rue Bourbon in New Orleans, my partner and I giggled at an ominous looking faux cat in an abandoned fortune-teller's window.

Brent's shoulder bumped into mine as he quickly swerved to the right to miss a group of firefighters just up ahead, who were laughing raucously. There seemed to be a lighter mood at the dawn of dusk and my steps bounced a little higher as we turned to pass the group.

Brent grabbed my hand to guide me around the group considering the fact that the sidewalk wasn't very large. I happened to glance back at the group as we passed to get a better look when I noticed them pointing degradingly at something across the street. Their laughter from moments before now caused a chill to sweep over me as I realized they were making fun of someone.

I paused in mid-step with Brent pulling on my hand to keep going. I ignored him for a moment to take a look at what the firemen were making fun of.

My stomach began to twist in contorting knots as I saw a gang of mixed Cajun men shoving each other around with sloppy grins on their faces. There was just something eerie that began to challenge the mood as my observation became stationary.

My first thought was...*Are these guys just having some fun and throwing playful punches at each other like guys commonly do...or is this the makings of a real fight?* I almost didn't want to know the answer but with sickening dread the reality of the matter painstakingly sank in.

I turned in slow motion to see the group of firemen just several feet from me making snide remarks and laughing with glee at the group of Cajuns. My lips pressed into a thin line and my eyes narrowed to slits as I looked back at the rowdy group of Cajuns.

I swallowed thickly as I saw a clearer picture of what was happening. There were five attackers, one main one, and a smaller-built man…the victim, who appeared Hispanic. The Cajuns were shoving him around, throwing punches, laughing and sneering at the smaller man. It was a five-men to one-man fight. *Yeah that seemed fair!* I shook my head in disgust and my hands clenched into fists at my sides.

"Rose, let's go." Brent said quickly trying to pull my hand away from my side. "It's not safe, we'd best leave." He continued hurriedly.

I turned around to glare at him still saying nothing.

My head whipped back to the fight across the street as a loud bone-splitting sound smashed into the cobblestone. I gasped in shock as I saw the victim lying flat on his back. We had just arrived at the moment the scene turned ugly. The firemen standing to the left abruptly stopped laughing and stared at the horrid scene in front of them.

The four attackers stepped back as the victim struggled to his feet as the fifth attacker viciously punched the man back. The man was so weak and defenseless at this point, the force of the blow literally lifted the victim's feet off the ground and his body flew straight back, his skull and spine once again smacking the cobblestone with a loud slap.

I froze for a moment wondering why everyone was just staring? Why wasn't anyone stopping this attack? My heart fluttered out of pace at the next thought. *Which blow would be the fatal one?* I knew from past research and experience that a single blow to the head could be a fatal one.

There is not much known about concussions or when too much trauma ultimately becomes too much for the brain to take. All that is known as far as the ultimatum for the brain's tolerance, is that it cannot take a lot of stressful blows…especially all in one setting.

In July of 2004, my car slipped into a dump-truck size pile of dirt left by the Road Commission, hidden right around a curve in a main road, with no warning signs posted. It caused my car to gain speed as it slipped down a hill, and then slam into a tree at 45 miles an hour, roof first. The accident fractured the left part of my skull, broke my left arm in three places, lacerated my body all over, and left me with a grade-3 concussion (the worst).

A mere six-months later, driving in Georgia, an elderly man ran a red light hitting me head-on leaving me with a second consecutive concussion, this one a Grade-1 severity. I was sent in for three months of testing with a neurologist, and received additional CAT scans and MRI's because of the unfortunate consistency of recent head trauma.

I was cleared with a clean bill of health and could only thank God for truly watching over me. On the flip side, I was banned from playing sports for a while, or any other rigorous activity that could onset another incidental concussion. The doctor said if I did get another concussion anytime soon, it would most likely be fatal.

Slipping back into the moment, I tried to quell my fears of the severity of head injuries for the targeted victim. I was terrified for the man's life. He would be dead soon just from the head trauma if this didn't stop. The victim struggled to his knees and slowly got to his feet once again. The main attacker laughed sneeringly, followed by his comrades, and gripped the man by the collar holding him up.

The man pulled back his fist and smashed the guy viciously again in the jaw sending the victim once again flying through the air, and the sound of his bones smacking the stone split the silence as the onlookers looked on stunned.

I was furious. I will never yell and scream at someone over a misunderstanding, over a relationship flaw, or even over harsh words said to me. I learned early on that harsh words once spoken can never be erased and the pain inflicted by them can never be forgotten. It is easy to ask for forgiveness, but impossible to erase the reason why you asked for it.

But I stand here today, and will say...I will NEVER settle for cruelty, for inhumane behavior, or any sort of injustice to mankind...especially to an innocent, helpless victim.

So let me tell you, if someone is standing there helpless, defenseless, being beaten to death in front of my eyes, being beaten by criminals, cruel men that can stand there and laugh at the victim's helplessness, literally crushing his bones with their vicious stikes...I REFUSE to stand for that sort of injustice. I REFUSE.

People as humans...yes, we fail in our everyday communications and have misunderstandings. We find out facts and move on. We don't beat each other and hate and fight. This is outlandishly childish and the complete coward's way out.

This was different and I will die fighting for justice, for what I believe in, to save another…even if it ends up being the last thing I do. There are already too many people standing on the sidelines waiting for someone else to make a difference, someone else to take a stand, and someone else to be the bigger person.

Nothing will ever change if we all stand around waiting for that someone. If that someone ever does come…it most likely will be too late anyways. We have to take a stand when it counts.

By this time, the main attacker had grabbed the victim by the neck for the last time. The victim was barely conscious, his eyes rolling back in his head, and his neck was hanging awkwardly to one side. I just moved. I didn't think. There was nothing left to think. Even more, there wasn't any more time left to think.

All I knew, was there was a fury within me that I had never felt before…with an even greater fury at the men standing to my left frozen in horror at the situation…not attempting at all to stop the assault. Five grown men could easily take on the five attackers. But nobody ever wants to involve themselves in other peoples' "business".

I quickly turned to glance at Brent and saw that he was standing there immobile, his face unmoving. My mind quickly started shouting at me…*Have you thought about weapons? Do the attackers have guns or knives hidden on them? What chance do you have against them anyways, 5-1?*

Well, according to my eyes…the attackers were using fists…and only one of them was truly fighting. I honestly didn't even care at that point if they did have a weapon because as it stood...I would DARE them to try to pull a gun on me...I'd dare them to try...and if they somehow managed to do just that, then I would take the bullet, but I was not going to let this victim be killed right in front of my eyes...I could NEVER live with that.

I'd rather die with the peace of knowing I'd given my all and tried my best, than to live with the regret of knowing I could have saved a man, but had been too scared, and that my cowardice had ultimately been the very death of him.

If the situation would have been switched around and I had been the victim of this assault, I would have loved for someone to be looking out for me. I would have died to have someone take a stand for me...to save me.

I was so furious. How could people just stand there and not help this poor, totally helpless man? Even worse, how could they let the attackers gleefully assault this man right in front of everyone...so arrogantly and boastfully? HOW???

I don't think I have ever been so furious in my life. Never have I seen myself that angry, nor anyone that knows me could imagine it. I dropped my stuff, letting it strew all over the sidewalk in a flutter of paperwork. I whipped around in fury and shouted,

"Why are you guys making ME do this?"

The next moment, my feet left the pavement and started charging over to the assailants. Brent and the firemen instantly turned to watch this new turn of events.

What happened next, happened in a slow-motion manner. Everyone froze in astonishment, watching this

100 lb. girl charging over to the attackers, fury, blatant fury that could not only be seen but felt.

Brent felt chills slither down his spine at the premonition that something bad was going to happen. The bystanders could only watch in horror…too terrified to speak, scream or yell.

I had no inhibitions and no fears…even now. I was on a mission, with a purpose, and all I knew was that I was going to stop this cruelty, and nothing, absolutely nothing would stop me from attaining that…NOTHING!

I don't swear. It isn't ladylike nor is it respectful in my eyes…but on this night…I did. I literally jumped right up in the attackers faces, shoving myself into their group, while the victim slumped to the ground, released by my blunt arrival as the assailants turned to face me.

My face was contorted in fury and my green eyes blazed hell. My blonde hair hung in long curls around my face with an eerie glow cast from the streetlight. My face was flushed red and my lips pressed in a tight expression of daringness.

I didn't pause. I stood on the tips of my toes trying to get right up in front of their eyes despite my 5'5" height, screaming,

"What the --- do you think you're doing? Get your --- hands off of him you filthy ---!"

The audacity for such a small girl like me to speak so harshly to someone so much more powerful…had everyone else watching, literally shaking in their boots or peeing their pants. My fists were pulled back daring them to challenge me…daring them to move…daring them to say ONE word.

The main attacker looked me straight in the eyes and swallowed quickly, his eyes opened wide…and in a moment of preponderance, it was as if the world stood still. Nobody moved in those few seconds…everyone could only hold their breath in this sudden showdown of sides.

I held my stare with the main attacker not flinching in the slightest bit. My gaze remained unwavering and the expression of fury on my face and was so fierce in its force that the main attacker actually backed up a step.

I was about to take a step forward when all five attackers, all wide-eyed now in shock, clearly unsure of what to do, turned abruptly and fled, leaving me there with my hands clenched in fists at my sides.

I think even I for a moment was surprised at how fast the situation had changed. I didn't have time to think anymore. I sank to the ground and straddled the victim. He was entirely motionless and the mere touch of his skin was as cold as ice.

His shirt was bunched up tightly around his neck and many chains twisted there from where the attacker had held him up by his throat. I ripped the chains and shirt back slipping my hands around his neck trying to find a pulse.

Upon my immediate attempt, I couldn't find one. My eyes clenched together to fight the emotion that threatened to overtake me. My breathing came in ragged gasps as I struggled to keep searching for a pulse.

The man's eyes were closed and his body remained completely motionless. My first impression of assessing the victim was that the life in him just seemed gone.

I didn't dare move any part of him for I knew the severe head trauma was the reason he was as lifeless as he was. There was no doubt in my mind that he had cervical and lumbar fractures as well. I didn't want to risk paralyzing him by moving any part of him that could risk damaging his spinal cord and causing further damage.

I couldn't find a pulse. I saw my hands move over his chest and felt my arms starting full-blown chest compressions. I glanced at the victim's face to see if there were any signs of life showing in response to my efforts...he remained motionless and unresponsive. I didn't stop. I couldn't.

I don't know what came over me but my prior First Aid training just automatically kicked in. I knew I had to save this man. I was praying so hard in those moments, I didn't notice at first the hands on my shoulders. I felt them, but didn't realize someone was talking to me.

I glanced up to notice an EMT standing over me trying to let me know they had arrived. I saw another two EMTs rushing up with First Aid supplies and a backboard. To my left was an ambulance, lights flashing and parked really close to where I crouched by the victim on the sidewalk.

I think it was in those moments that shock started to set in, and I quickly shook my head trying to fight it and heard myself saying,

"I couldn't find a pulse. I have been doing chest compressions..." I paused as one of the EMT's took over the compressions for me. Another paramedic took one of the man's arms and started to get an IV in him.

"He needs a neck brace, and complete stabilization on the back board. He's suffered extreme blunt force trauma to his entire body, but significantly to his skull and entire spine." I just kept talking and stopped when I heard one of the EMT's exclaim,

"I've got a pulse."

I suddenly felt extreme relief and was about to say a silent prayer of thanks, when the sound of police sirens distracted me once again. I stepped back, climbing weakly to my feet as I turned to face the police officer that had just arrived on the scene.

I didn't even wait for him to speak. My mind now was racing a million miles a minute and I reached out and grabbed the officer's arm and started pulling him down the sidewalk, urging him to run. I was following him for a short bit as I hurriedly explain the attack. I stopped running, repeating over and over,

"They went that way. The attackers went that way. Go."

The officer never even got a word in. He nodded and started running down the sidewalk in the direction the assailants had fled. He was shouting into his radio calling in for backup as I watched him disappear down the street.

I was about to follow him, when several more cop cars flew up to the scene, sirens blaring and multiple officers jumped out and began to scour the area for the attackers.

I didn't know which way to turn then. This was my battle. I always used to wonder why the good guy in all those murder mystery novels would stop and help the fallen victim first before going after the attackers.

I always thought, wouldn't it be easier to find the attacker's first so that they would stop killing people and in this way end up saving more lives…trusting that the current victim would survive his or her injuries...because as it comes to be, the victim is usually always ok...and the bad guys always get away.

I mean it is like this in the books at least. But no, no, no...that is not how it is. In real life, you help the fallen man first. That was my first instinct and even though I still berate myself for not following the attackers and giving them a taste of what it felt like to be victimized...I ultimately can and never will regret my initial decision.

I heard shouts to my left and turned back to see the three paramedics holding the victim down as his body convulsed unconsciously with a violent seizure. *Oh no!* The extent of his head injuries was already way too clear.

It wasn't until a half hour later that the man was stabilized enough to get into the ambulance. He was strapped onto the headboard and lifted onto a stretcher and transported into the back of the ambulance.

I swallowed quickly as the driver closed the doors on the back of the vehicle and hurriedly rushed up to the front to head to the hospital. I could see the heads of the other two EMT's through the back door windows rushing around the victim, who was not within my view anymore. Sirens started blaring as the ambulance pulled away and I heard someone coming up fast behind me.

"Ma'am, are you ok?"

It was the original police officer that had showed up to the scene that I had sent off in the direction of the assailants. I didn't really process his question in that moment and heard myself asking,

"Did you get them? Did you find the attackers?"

"We captured the main one, the ringleader based on the description you gave. We need you to ID him."

I was shocked and a small glimmer of hope engulfed me in that moment…that there was a chance that justice would still be served. The arrest of this man lay in my hands. In order for the officers to book him, they had to have a witness to verify his crimes. I swallowed thickly and said,

"Bring me to him."

I followed the officer a couple of streets down to where a tall, dark-haired man was being read his rights and handcuffed next to a police car.

The attacker happened to turn just then and looked me straight in the eyes. I didn't flinch for a moment as I slowly nodded my head and calmly said,

"That's him. That's the man."

It was in that moment I felt no glee or patronizing pleasure at seeing the man caught. It was pity I felt for him...pity for the sad, cruel life that a criminal lives. So much pain and loss that it ends up being, and the most heartbreaking thing about it all is that they have no one to blame but themselves.

Well, at this point I was praying that the victim wouldn't die from internal bleeding, brain damage, or any of his horrific injuries. I really needed him to live, because he didn't deserve to die like this. Furthermore, I would all of the sudden be a key witness to a homicide and then...I don't want to think about what that would entail.

I turned and walked away, slowly heading back to the crime scene, looking up to see Brent heading my way. No words were spoken as he reached out and engulfed me in a huge hug, holding me in the security of his arms.

"That was a brave thing you did Rose," he said quietly. "You'd better not ever do that again," he finished with a small smile. "You really had us all scared." He paused for a moment, "I thought you were dead."

I just looked at him with an all-knowing smile that said, I'll be fine, and yes, I will still make my own decisions in the future, but thanks for your concern.

He let out a deep sigh knowing all too well I was serious.

The one image that keeps playing over and over in my mind, is the force in which the victim was attacked and flying through the air; the splitting sound of his bones and skull smacking cobblestone. You don't forget that sound. You don't forget the looks on the assailant's faces nor the pure glee they felt in inflicting such cruelty. It would be many weeks before I would be able to close my eyes not hear the sounds.

I am not overly emotional about this situation...it is more of striving to be strong. These are the situations that we are up against on an operation such as a Category 5 hurricane devastation...and these are what we must overcome.

Overall, I feel I handled the situation very accurately...and even the police we're amazed at my courage to act upon fighting for what is right. They were utterly shocked that I was the only one that took a stand, and thanked me profusely for being one of the good guys...never once chiding me for putting myself at risk, which I greatly appreciated.

There are thousands of Americans that put their lives at risk on a daily basis, from firefighters, to police officers, to special agents, to military personnel...and many more. Just because I am a linguist, a normal citizen, doesn't mean I too, shouldn't be willing to put my life on the line for this country.

It is our freedom in which we all fight for, <u>and the true hero, is the person that recognizes the responsibility that comes along with his or her freedom.</u> We are a nation, and we are all in this together, so we must stick together and stay together.

All in all, as hard as it is to believe, all was going well. In a sense, it was simply a kaleidoscope of constant crises in which we strived to control, contain and also correlate with the correct authorities to handle them.

This was our job here, and I couldn't think of anything I'd rather be doing. As arduous, dangerous and unstable the circumstances were here, I felt underneath all that a comfortable peace one would feel at home.

The fieldwork, crime, sickness, fatigue, the devastation of it all didn't faze me, because there was something deeper inside that meant more to me than all of the obstacles that could bring me down...and that "something more" was making all the difference.

Thinking back, my mom once told me, "Rosie, if you ever meet a terrorist, it will be the terrorist who is scared of you, never you of them." She never once fears for me when I travel because she trusts my ability to take care of myself. And to an extent, as much as we can control a situation ourselves, it's true.

Everyone on the street that day will testify to the force that I had in which I attempted and strived to save that man's life. He was dead when I got to him; his heart had stopped beating. I kept him alive with CPR until help arrived. I'll never forget those moments.

<u>If you don't stand for something, you'll fall for anything.</u> Someone has to do something. I don't wait around for others to make a difference. It'll never happen. If I am the only one that tries, then I'll be the only one that tries. However, I am willing to fight to the death to stand for what's right, because this country has slipped too far below it's privileges, and we need people to start taking a stand to fight for the freedom that was granted this country so long ago. We are losing that vision because of our selfishness.

There are too many evil people hurting the innocent, too many crooked cops taking advantage of civilians, too many selfish criminals using disasters as a means to accomplish an even bigger, more evil scheme. America, let's rise up, and make a difference. Let's be the change we want to see in the world.

TUESDAY, OCTOBER 11th
ROBBED
3:05 A.M.

The night was still and a pale moon cast an eerie glow upon this quiet part of town. I parked the car at the motel a little too exhausted to care or notice. I turned off the ignition and let my head rest on the steering wheel with the last notes of my trip theme song, "This is How a Heart Breaks", drift off into the night.

My eyes slowly closed as I let my racing thoughts battle each other in my head, and tried to drown them out. I felt in that moment a strange overwhelming feeling hit me. All of the recent events felt like they were catching up to me and in that small moment of quiet I felt an extra force extracting more of my strength.

I let out a deep, long sigh and forced a weak smile urging myself on. I slipped my keys out of the ignition, grabbed my backpack and wearily climbed out of the car. I closed the door quietly, turned and locked it behind me.

There was a strange silence over the parking lot and an absence of sound that normally would have engaged my senses. Yet on this night, I could only think of making it to my motel room and falling onto the bed.

I climbed the stairs warily, plodding one foot in front of the other. Peering into the blackness, I haphazardly felt for the knife at my hip for reassurance. My backpack slipped off my shoulder, and I stumbled briefly for a moment on the long set of stairs leading up to the second floor. I couldn't see anything it was so dark, and the electricity was still out in the stairwell. I turned the corner and slid my card into the motel door. The little red light blinked back at me mockingly, and I glanced nervously over my shoulder at the delay. I quickly shoved my card in again and cleanly pulled it out. *Finally!* The light flashed green, and I hurriedly snuck into my room.

I dropped my bag, lifted my badge over my head and placed it on the desk. I turned the desk light on so that I could see where I was going. The room was full of shadows, and the curtains were closed and hanging still. I looked at the bed. The sheets were in the same position that I had left them earlier this morning.

The comforter was still crumpled in a pile with the pillows hiding under it. The garbage to my right still had trash filling it and it looked as if no new towels had been brought because the used ones from last night still lay in a damp pile outside the bathroom door.

The lampshade to the right of the bed suddenly caught my attention. My body stiffened as I noticed the shade tilted at a strange angle. I slowly moved around the side of the bed, my lips frozen together in a trance of sudden suspicion.

My eyes widened as I quickly noticed my phone charger missing from it's resting place on the nightstand. I never moved the charger. I left it plugged in all day and all night and in the same place on the nightstand every day. I had never moved it since I had arrived. I paused. *Was somebody here? Was somebody in the same room with me right now...hiding?*

My exhaustion was forgotten in that moment. My weariness fled and I went around the bed quickly, my hand slipping down to my knife. I quickly went to the front door locked it. I moved quietly though, as to not let the thief know that I knew of his or her crime yet! If someone was here, they weren't leaving until they had a word with me!

I turned off the lights and started to hum a song nonchalantly. *They wouldn't just take my phone charger...they would have taken everything,* I thought.

My eyes whipped back to the desk and noticed all of my belongings completely gone except for the badge I just placed on it. *Now I was beginning to get furious! What was happening?* I strode angrily over to the bathroom and kicked the door open, flipping the light on all in the same motion. *Nothing! I wasn't going to be fooled though, I* thought.

I went inside the bathroom and brashly pulled back the shower curtain. *Nothing!* I went back to the bedroom and slipped to the floor looking underneath the bed. *I swear if the person who had taken my things was still here, they were going to wish they had never messed with me!* The bed was empty. *Again nothing!*

My motel room was vacant. No one was here. The thief was gone and so were all my belongings that I had left in my motel room. Even my glasses were gone. *How was I going to see if I lost one of my contacts? I am completely blind without either! Oh no!*

I tripped over my backpack still lying in the middle of the floor as I discouragingly went over to the edge of the bed. I backed onto it slowly, letting out a weakened sigh. *Why? Why did this have to happen to me?*

I leaned back on the bed letting my head rest on the rumpled comforter. I stared at the ceiling with a complete look of devastation. I was frustrated, hurt, and most of all angry. *Who had done this? Why? How could someone have gotten into my motel room?* Wait that was just it! On second thought, I quickly got up and went over to the window. I pulled back the curtains and felt the locks. I frowned realizing they were still in place and the glass was not broken. *They had to have come in with a key!*

I went back over to the bed and sat down, this time holding my head in my hands. I took my knife off my hip and laid it next to me on the bed. *It had to have been someone that was still working at the motel!* It had to have been. *There is no other way they would have had access to a key to my room.*

Actually, it was probably the same person that put new towels in my room everyday! I let out a huff. *Now that was comforting!* In that moment, I was so frustrated I didn't know what to do. I didn't feel safe anymore, even being locked inside my motel room.

The adrenaline of the situation still masked my exhaustion but I felt my frustration weakening my resolve to keep my head up. *How dare someone steal from me! What had I done to them? Nothing!* Oh wait, but I had.

I had come from hundreds of miles away from the northern state of Michigan to the southern incapacitated state of Louisiana to help the victims of the largest catastrophic natural disaster to ever hit the U.S. I came to help people that I didn't even know…people that I would never see again…and people that could never do anything to return the favor.

Even more, I had come to help the very person that had stolen my things. I had come to help his or her people. And in return, I had gotten robbed blindly behind my back. It was a cold blow and it really pierced my heart.

   I grabbed my knife, put it on the night table, flipped off the lights and wearily crawled under the covers. I closed my eyes trying to shut out the discouraging thoughts of the evening.

   Suddenly, something came over me and I bolted upright. I tilted my head in puzzlement as I let the realization unfold. My attitude was all wrong I realized. *Who was I to judge?* If you do what you've always done, you'll get what you've always got. Thus, getting angry and frustrated would not solve anything, it never did.

   It would not change the fact that my belongings were gone and it certainly would not bring them back. Retaliation would only entail more horrible things to happen. *What if there really was a solution to this?* What if miracles really did happen and what if I could really reverse the whole situation? Not the cops, not the authorities, not the hotel management...but me?

   It is as if a light bulb had gone off, and I suddenly had a visual in a dark room. What if there was a chance that perhaps everything in life that happened to us would only cause us defeat if we settled for it? What if we chose to not settle for the norm? What if we chose to not settle for defeat? What if we chose to not settle for the expected? What if we rose above that possibility, option, or probability and had faith that rose above reason itself? Faith, that we could truly change the world around us?

   What if the defeats in our lives only remained defeats as long as we accepted them? What if we chose to deny the defeats and somehow could change them into successes? What if there was a way? The end is only the end when we accept it as the end, right?

As long as there is hope, there is a vision for change. I didn't even know how to explain these thoughts that went through my mind at this time. It was just this unseen force that was pushing me into a different direction than I had intended to go. And, I went with it because it captivated me.

I believe that beyond our human intelligence and capability, there is something so much greater that has the final say in every situation. God. We are only human…and because of that we are very much imperfect. I was curious to see where this newfound realization was taking me.

I turned on the lamp next to me and suddenly it hit me. One of my favorite quotes popped into my mind and I knew. *"You see things; and say, WHY? I see things thought impossible; and I say, WHY NOT?"* (by George Bernard Shaw) This was one of those situations. *WHY NOT?*

The impossible is only deemed impossible as long as you let it be improbable. Something new that has never been done or accomplished before will never be a reality until someone decides to say WHY NOT and make it happen.

It was then that I knew what I had to do. *WHY NOT?* There was only defeat as long as I was going to accept it. My whole attitude was changing and my heart started to soften a bit. I slipped my feet into the other person's shoes, the person that had stolen my belongings.

From what I had discovered of Louisiana and the interactions of society here, I realized that a lot of people just plain survived by stealing, robbing and doing other petty crimes or worse. (Even before the hurricane had hit.)

What if per chance, the person that had stolen my things was just trying to get by, to survive through the horrible aftermath of Katrina? What if they didn't even realize that I had come to help them and their fellow neighbors?

Well, if my inclination was right, then what I was about to do next would prove it. I tore a small piece of paper off a notepad I'd found in the drawer of the nightstand and penned a short, simple heartfelt message.

It read as follows:

Dear Friend,

I write this note to let you know that today I realized several of my things were missing. I just wanted you to know that I have come all the way from Michigan without pay to help you and your people get back on your feet after the hurricane. If perchance you knew where my belongings went... it would mean the world to me if they could be returned. Many thanks.

God Bless You,

Rosemary Martin

Safety and Security
The Red Cross

I was very careful with the way the note was worded and I refrained from implying in any way that my items had been stolen. Further, I was sure to include the fact that I only wanted to HELP, and that being my purpose here. I felt confident that the message was clear, yet considerate and kind too.

I placed the handwritten note on the desk for it to be found the next morning. If all of my assumptions were right and the person that worked for the motel helping out with the upkeep of the rooms was the culprit of this crime, then tomorrow I would know. Even more, if they had stolen out of carelessness and not maliciousness...perhaps the impossible could be realized here and my things could be returned.

I went to bed then, this time with peace in my heart and happiness that I had handled the situation with kindness and not hatred.

WEDNESDAY, OCTOBER 12th
THE VERDICT
1:00 A.M.

The following day, I went about my duties and the handwritten note lying on the desk in my motel room slipped to the back of my mind. It wasn't until my weary self was slipping the card key into the motel door again at 1:00 in the morning that I remembered the note. I frowned then, feeling a hint of wariness, expecting the note to be lying there still, forgotten and ignored.

I slowly opened the front door, using my left hand to slip the light on. I walked in, concentrating on setting down my backpack and slipping off my shoes before working up the courage deal with the note on the desk.

I pressed my lips firmly together in their normal stance of preparedness and walked slowly over to the desk. I paused in mid-step as my eyes found the desktop. *What?*

My jaw dropped open and hung there, my throat tightening in shock. I swallowed thickly not believing what I saw. I was even more surprised at the emotion that assailed me then and several tears began to well up in my eyes.

Lying there on the desktop was every single one of my missing belongings...the note was gone...and in replacement was a short note of apology!

I left my mouth hanging agape not knowing what to do. *How could it be? Was this for real? Was it just me, or did a robbery just happen...and then miraculously the robber return the stolen goods? Had* this ever *happened before?* My secret plan had worked! What a miracle!

As absurd as this story may seem…it really isn't that far-fetched. People will only live as they are taught, and a lot of people here have only been taught that it is ok to resort to crime to survive…it is no different than the little children out in the Middle East that are taught to hate Americans from their youth.

How will someone know any different unless someone takes the TIME to TEACH them a NEW way? A better way? A kinder way? The right way?

FRIDAY, OCTOBER 14th
CONGRESSIONAL COORESPONDENCE
5:35 P.M.

Today was the day I received the most shocking email of my life. But before I get into what the email said, there are some other things that I have to explain first. A brief interlude into my past will better explain the initiation of this email. I will begin when I was 16 years old.

Ever since I was a young girl, I have been very passionate about doing public service for this country. I started at the age of 16 working every public election thus far for the local government back in my hometown of Fenton for Tyrone Township.

Two years later, after being an election inspector for two years, the year I was legally allowed to vote for the first time, I began training to coordinate an election. Shortly after that, I was awarded the position to run entire elections all by myself as the Deputy Registrar for the Township.

In addition, since 1997, I have been doing non-profit volunteer work for Send the Light Outreach (as previously mentioned) whose mission is to assist those spiritually and physically in Central America as well as so many countries around the world.

When I turned 17, I started teaching English as a Second Language to new incoming foreign students in the Hartland Consolidated School District, using my already competent skills in foreign languages and linguistics. It was at this age that I wrote my first novel...a spy thriller!

By the age of 18, I was deep into my studies of six foreign languages and shadowing a court interpreter to enhance my interpreting skills and become qualified to court interpret on my own.

When I turned 19, I started my own business as a linguist, interpreting, translating, and instructing foreign languages. Soon after, I began interpreting in the Howell Courts in Michigan using my well-traveled Spanish skills.

I then turned down a job offer from the NSA (National Security Agency) to be a language analyst, so that I would be able to continue my linguistic efforts in my hometown in Michigan where they are so desperately needed.

Five months later, I enlisted with the Red Cross to assist with the Hurricane Katrina relief efforts in August of 2005, as you are now reading about. So now you are caught up to speed.

So, having said all that, I was in between meetings when I decided to check my email really quickly to kill a few minutes. I was shocked to see an email from a liaison to Mike Rogers, our current Republican Congressman representing Michigan in Washington D.C.

My hands were shaking a little as I clicked on the message to open it. At this moment, everything else in the room was tuned out...every person, every sound, every action...they all became a muted cloud around me. For some reason, before the email opened, I had a good feeling about it.

The message populated on the screen and read like this:

Dear Rosie,

    It is my pleasure to know you. I am grateful and inspired with your commitment to assist in the relief efforts. Your dedication to public service is commendable. I think we should send you a tribute. I certainly will let Congressman Rogers know who you are, and what you are doing and I hope to meet you some day. You are a true patriot. I hope to hear from you soon.

Be safe,

S.

It was just a short paragraph, but so powerful nonetheless. The sentence that caught my attention the most was: "You are a true patriot." Never in my life have I received a compliment as great as that.

It was as if my vision for my life had already been recognized and so quickly understood and respected! It was the first time I didn't feel alone in my desire to support this country, nor in finding ways to give back and help the country as well.

That email was a ray of sunshine that just sort of made me feel something inside that said, *"Yes, it truly was meant for you to be on the Operation...and more than that, your efforts have not gone unnoticed or unappreciated."* It was those last thoughts that gave me the strength to endure until the end of my deployment.

SUNDAY, OCTOBER 16TH
THE ASSAULT (#2)
7:09 P.M.

Today was the day that I would happen upon another violent assault. It was later in the day and I was in New Orleans with Brent.

We were just about to leave the city and head back to Baton Rouge when once again we were standing on the street corner waiting to cross the street when the sound of shattering glass caused both of us to freeze.

I turned quickly to the right, just in time to see a beer bottle crashing through a pale blue pick-up truck back-seat window, bringing along with it a rain of glass shards. The shower of glass seemed to freeze momentarily in the air and fall almost in slow motion as I let my senses quickly absorb the entire situation.

I could see a middle-aged man wearing a dark baseball cap leaning over the front seat of the truck to make contact with another similar-aged man wearing a red and white plaid shirt. His fists pummeled the other guy, pushing him even further into the backseat of the vehicle.

The truck was several car-lengths away from where Brent and I stood so it was hard to see the exact damage being done.

Having so recently been forced to deal with another violent assault, I didn't even think this time. My feet slipped off the sidewalk onto the street almost routinely, my arms hanging steady by my sides.

My body jerked forward abruptly as I felt my feet skid to a stop in mid-step. My head and hair whipped back. I turned quickly, gasping as I felt a small pain in my wrist and noticed Brent clamping his hand over mine. He quickly reached up and grabbed my other hand, pulling me roughly over to him.

"No Rose. It's not your fight." He said gruffly.

I turned and looked Brent in the eyes, begging for him to let me go. He stared back at me unmoving, the piercing blue of his eyes momentarily freezing me. He was serious.

"No way! Let me go! I exclaimed. "Brent, I swear let me go! You can't just stand there and let this man be beaten!"

"I don't care what you say, I am not letting you go! You will get hurt if you go over there."

I ignored his sensibility and tried to break free of his grasp. He pulled me close and engulfed me in a friendly vise.

The sound of another beer bottle smashing onto the pavement caused both of us to look quickly back at the scene of the ongoing attack. *Where are all these beer bottles coming from?* I used the momentary distraction to slip free of Brent's hold and quickly headed over towards the truck.

"Rose, no!" He shouted standing there with his hands outstretched towards me. I ignored his pleas and grimaced as I watched the guy in the front seat of the truck smash a beer bottle right into the second guy's face in the backseat. The man's face spun to the left and tottered back and forth for a few moments before collapsing sideways on the back seat.

Ohh, that made me so angry!

"HEY!" I shouted.

The attacker glanced up just then, surprised for a brief moment to see a tiny blond-haired girl shouting at him. He didn't pause long though, and before I had shouted my next threatening, "HEY!" he had pushed open the passenger-side door and leapt onto the sidewalk, fleeing the scene just as I skidded up to the side of the truck, my feet crunching over the shards of glass littering the roadway. *Why are people so stupid? Did punching a guy in the face till he collapsed truly solve anything?*

Since it was only a two-door pick-up, I had to pry open the driver's-side door to get to the victim. I did my best to maneuver around all the pieces of broken glass and winced as a sliver grazed my left hand as I placed it on the front seat while trying to pull myself up into the truck.

Why did I feel like I was always the ONLY one around that was willing to take a stand and do the right thing? Why did everyone either just plain not care or let fear hold them back? What was there to lose?

If the roles were reversed and someone had been attacking or beating me and I was unable to defend myself, I know I would be hoping someone would step in and help me! It was complete madness here! There was no control anywhere.

Crime was rampant and commonplace. There were not enough police officers available to handle the flood of violence that ensued after Katrina, and the ones available could not always be trusted. There was no higher power in charge that would hold anyone accountable- police or foe for the most part, thus allowing havoc to be routine.

The victim let out a gurgled gasp and a thin line of blood trickled from his lips, running slowly down the side of his jawbone.

I could see him then, barely...but enough. The evening shadows were closing in and cloaked him in a blanket of darkness. His eyes were open, blinking rapidly as he tried to focus on me.

I think my rapid movements were making me dizzy, because he started to pinch his eyes shut and his breath was very labored. Either that, or his head trauma was severe enough to be causing the dizziness and sensitivity to light and quick movements.

"Help," he muttered weakly.

"It's ok. I got you. Just lie still." I said calmly. I reached over the seat and let my hands find the pulse on his neck. My hand slipped over something wet and sticky as I tried to keep my hand steady on his neck.

"Try to hold still, I'm gonna take care of you." I said calmly with confidence. His pulse was steady and strong. *Good.*

It was too hard to assess his injuries with him lying in the backseat of a tiny truck. We had to get him out but I really didn't want to do that without an EMT, because I couldn't be sure he didn't need a neck brace or back support before he could be moved safely. I would have to crawl in the back somehow. I needed to stop the bleeding.

"Rose, what's going on? How is he?" Brent said suddenly from my right. I turned to see him standing next to the truck holding the driver's door open. I frowned at him briefly before replying.

"He looks alright. Stable. His pulse is strong and I think most of his wounds are superficial from being hit with the bottles. He seems to have a significant laceration on his right temple that will need stitches."

"I really want to put pressure on it to stop the bleeding but I can't get to him around all the glass. Why don't you go find an EMT and have them take over for us. I'll stay here and watch him until you get back."

"But—" Brent started to say and I cut him off. "Hurry!" I said turning away from him.

I leaned back over the seat looking back at the victim. I wish I had something sterile to use to stop the bleeding. It wasn't life threatening so I didn't proceed any further with it for the moment.

"Help is on the way, just hang in there buddy, ok?" I said with an encouraging smile even though I knew he couldn't see me that clearly. His left arm went out and he tried to prop himself up.

"Hey, hey, hey, let me help you!" I said quickly. I leaned further in and placed my hands under his armpits so that he could prop himself up into a sitting position.

The stench of beer and blood seared my nostrils, and I coughed roughly trying not to breathe in. I winced as I felt another shard of glass scratching through the material of my shirt into my abdomen. Ignoring it, I reached over to brush the shards of glass off the victim's lap and made sure he could sit up on his own before I let go of him.

I didn't have anything to wipe the blood off of his face, but didn't have to wonder a moment longer because just then, Brent returned with two EMT's in tow.

"Alright, ma'am we'll take it from here," one of the burly paramedic's said.

"Thank you," I said turning to climb down from the truck. I glanced back at the victim really quickly and said, "Good luck, Sir."

As Brent and I headed away and the light of the street lamps cleared my vision, I noticed bright, red blood covering my hands and the front of my shirt. My eyes widened for a moment, slightly shocked. That explained the wet, stickiness I'd felt when I had been checking the victim's pulse.

"Whoa, you need to get that off!" Brent said quickly, noticing the blood in the same moment.

"I didn't even notice!" I said. "C'mon, we have to go find water." I said heading back into the direction of town.

After going to several bars and restaurants that were open, we found out that none of them had any running water. It was all contaminated. *Oh no!* (Mind you, they were only selling beer and liquor because it was the only sanitary thing to drink in New Orleans!)

I ended up having to go into the bathroom and temporarily wash the blood off my arms and hands with a bottle of hand sanitizer. The room was so dimly lit, I couldn't even see if I was really making this situation any better or not. *Less blood or more blood?* I couldn't tell.

I'd have to shower and scrub it off "better" back in Baton Rouge in my dirty bathtub with the spider.

And that was that. All in a day's work as they say, right? At least when there was the opportune moment to make a difference, I took it. For as certain as the sun shines, once that opportune moment has vanished, so has your chance.

TUESDAY, OCTOBER 18th
ANDERSON COOPER, CNN
7:00 P.M.

I successfully out-processed today and handed my position over to my replacement. It felt so great to hand over all of my hard work in setting up the Staff Shelters and the system we had put in place to keep them running safely and efficiently.

It felt like progress, like I had literally "as one human being", had made a difference in some very important way on this incredibly huge Operation!

I decided that because I was off-duty, I would head back to New Orleans that evening, this time just to see the city. I took Brent with me for security and ended up leaving for the city around 7:00 in the evening. Little did I know, that a few hours later I would be conversing with Anderson Cooper in Swahili.

It is so ironic sometimes the things that happen in life. The future is a tapestry that is constantly being woven with the present. But at the same time, the past can link to the present or the future. Even more, no matter what the connections are in timing, the only thing that truly stands is the present! What is currently happening at the current moment!

One of my dear friends from back in high school, Hanh, made a strange comment to me before I left Michigan. She said, "Rosemary, you are going to be on TV again!" And then she laughed with her little teasing all-knowing smile.

I let out a huff, *no way!* I raised an eyebrow and looked at her and said, "No, seriously there is no way that will happen." And I blew off the comment and didn't think any more of it.

Little did I know that she was right, because as Brent and I headed into New Orleans that night, so was CNN…and just perchance we were going to run into each other again.

We headed into the French Quarter, the evening stars dazzling like tiny diamonds amidst a black expanse of dark velvet. Music could be heard playing inside the different bars lining Bourbon Street, and bright lights lit up the town again.

The atmosphere was joyful, and the recent reopening of the town had enlightened a spirit of celebration and happiness as the residents and relief work personnel united in an unspoken toast to a new beginning.

Smiles were on everyone's faces, and even Mardi Gras beads were being thrown from balconies and street corners in reminiscence of what the French Quarter had been before Katrina and in defiance at how the French Quarter would survive even after her wrath.

Brent and I shook our heads at each other, surprised at how quickly things were changing here on the Relief Operation. We headed into a bar to grab a drink. The only food being made here was pizza, which tasted like cardboard, that we were also warned NOT TO EAT!

It still was unsanitary to be making food and using any water, so nothing was to be trusted except bottled or packaged stuff.

"This is a change," I murmured to Brent raising my eyebrow.

"Yeah, I don't think the spirit of New Orleans will ever die," he said with a smile. "C'mon, let's get a drink and go walk around some more!" He said and playfully nudged me in the shoulder.

"Ok, ok!" I said with a wide grin and nudged him back. We grabbed a couple of drinks called "Hurricanes". These were the main drink of choice right now of course, and basically the equivalent of three Long Island Iced Teas. *Very strong!* We headed back outside onto Bourbon Street.

To the left of where we stood, we could see a large crowd gathering on the next corner up. All we could see were a bunch of bright lights and a large throng of people, but the excitement was felt from even where we stood.

"Let's go!" I said quickly heading in that direction.

We reached the excited crowd and immediately could feel the electrifying pulse of anticipation.

"What's going on?" I asked inquisitively. Brent looked around trying to see over the people in front of us to find out what they were looking at. I wasn't tall enough to see over everyone. *What was going on?* Everyone was laughing and toasting their drinks with each other, and still more and more beads were being tossed everywhere.

"Brent, put me up on your shoulders so I can see!" I shouted over the commotion.

"Alright, here hold my drink," he said stooping down onto his knees.

I quickly hopped onto his back and just as Brent was lifting me up, one of the guys standing next to us who was wearing a blue baseball cap said, "Aww, aren't you two cute!" He laughed.

I smiled rolling my eyes. Brent stood up and I was just about to say, "Turn to the right", so I could see better when someone shouted, "Rosemary, is that you!"

I turned to the left and a big bright light was flashed in my face and a microphone shoved under my chin. My mouth was agape. It was Ben Blake with CNN!!! He had just interviewed me for CNN six months prior in Atlanta, Georgia about my job offer with the National Security Agency! *Oh my goodness! What was he doing here in New Orleans?*

"Hey, how are you!" I shouted, my face lighting up with the most enormous smile possible. *And we were LIVE on TV!* "What are you doing here?" I asked in surprise tilting my head.

Now this looks great, I thought. Last time I saw Ben, we were doing a very serious government piece for CNN, and here I was off duty in New Orleans on some guy's shoulders trying to look at something that I didn't even know what it was...still.

"What are you doing here?" Ben said with just as shocked of a smile.

"I just finished my deployment with the Red Cross doing Safety and Security on the Operation!" I replied.

"But you live in Michigan!" He said.

"And you live in Atlanta!" I replied laughing.

It was so ironic that I kept running into him everywhere possible except the state in which I was actually from! It certainly appeared as if I was never in Michigan...the state where I lived!

"How are you?" I asked.

"Great! I'm doing some coverage of Katrina." He explained. "Hey, can I interview you really quick?" He continued smiling, still holding the camera in my face.

I let out a laugh. "Just like old times!" I said winking. "Sure!" I nodded eagerly. At this point, I was still sitting on top of Brent's shoulders, the poor guy! And now, here was Ben going to interview me just like that.

By now, the crowd had turned and was watching me sit atop some guy's shoulders being interviewed by CNN. I know the people within earshot of our group were probably wondering how this random girl just casually new major CNN reporters. It was all very surreal!

The microphone was placed close to my face and the cameraman gave me the sign that we were rolling again. Neither Ben nor I could stop smiling. It was such a random act of fate, and we just rolled with it.

And so it began.

Ben introduced himself, explaining that he was covering the new nightlife of the French Quarter now that it had just been reopened for its citizens to return to the city. (The evacuation ban from the Hurricane had just been lifted). He went on to explain he was now interviewing one of the relief aides.

"What brought you to New Orleans?" He asked me first.

I slipped into serious mode and put on my best professional face as I entered into the interview.

"I came down here with the Red Cross to work with Safety and Security on the Relief Operation."

"Where are you originally from?" He asked for the benefit of the public, who didn't know this information.

"I'm from Michigan!" I said smiling widely.

What made you decide to join the relief efforts?" Ben continued.

I paused for a mere second before replying. "Honestly, I came down here to help, because I wanted to somehow, some way, make a difference for those who so desperately needed help getting back on their feet." I said simply and sincerely.

The interview went on for a few short minutes more and then was quickly wrapped up. As soon as the camera stopped recording I asked, "Ben, what are all of these people waiting for here?"

"Anderson Cooper is going LIVE in about twenty minutes." He said. "Go meet him! Tell him I sent you over." He said noticing my surprise.

Wow! I did want to meet Anderson. I wanted to know which languages he spoke! I looked back and noticed a small stage set with all the lighting and cameras, and teleprompter all prepped and ready to roll.

I quickly said thank you and goodbye to Ben Blake, and he headed off to interview more people. Brent and I pushed our way to the front of the crowd to the roped off section surrounding the stage. Security was tight, and I smiled sweetly at them as they noticed us closing in upon the stage.

I could see Anderson Cooper then. His back was to me, and he was looking at the teleprompter reviewing his lines.

"Hey, set me down," I told Brent.

I hopped to the ground and stood next to Brent taking in the scene. Excitement filled the air, and the crowd of people pressed forward, everyone trying to get a good view of the LIVE television cast.

"Wow, can you believe this?" I said looking at Brent. "This is really cool!"

"I know, it's amazing how we keep running into the craziest things every time we come into New Orleans!" Brent exclaimed. "I mean, I can't believe you knew that reporter! How often does that happen?"

"I know! I know it's so funny because I met him in Atlanta and I did a story for him and they aired it on CNN saying that I was all the way from Michigan. Then all of the sudden, I run into him again in New Orleans, both of us traveling from our home states and meeting again in another part of the country!"

I glanced back at Anderson Cooper and watched him turn and look right at me. I paused momentarily then, smiled and nodded my head at him in an unspoken greeting. He glanced quickly at security, waited for their nods of approval and then turned and headed directly toward me.

I reached out my hand to shake his, again this entire time a huge smile plastered on my face.

"Ben Blake sent me over here. My name is Rosemary Martin," I said, "Safety and Security with the Red Cross. It is a pleasure to meet you."

"Where are you from?" He asked kindly.

"I'm from Michigan." I said proudly.

"What do you do?" He asked me next.

"I'm a linguist, a self-employed language contractor. I speak six languages."

"Wow," he said, and I could tell he was surprised and very impressed.

"I'm studying Swahili right now," I added, just not even thinking or even realizing it had come out of my mouth till I saw his face do a double-take.

"Oh yes, I speak Swahili too!" Cooper said eagerly.

I quickly blurted out some Swahili that I'd learned in my recent studies and Anderson responded in turn.

It was like in that moment we had a common connection. The kind you can only have with people that speak foreign languages. I can't explain it. But I have felt it many times in my life, and it is just such an amazing feeling.

"Oh my goodness, did you learn it when you went to Africa?" I asked in surprise.

"No, I actually learned it in school, at the University!"

"Wow, you don't hear that often, I'm really surprised...and impressed!" I said. "Good for you! You're totally weird like me!" I added before I could realize that might come out wrong.

He laughed and shook his head in agreement. "Yeah, I get it. We're weird...but in a good way."

Someone called out, "Anderson, you're on again in five."

"It was a pleasure," he said giving me a hug, and then headed back to the set to go LIVE from the French Quarter.

SATURDAY, OCTOBER 22ND
RETURNING HOME
8:40 P.M.

My final email sent home:

Dear All,

I'm here preparing to depart Louisiana. I was scheduled to leave on Thursday, October 20th, but could not get a confirmed flight out until Saturday, October 22nd, which is in fact tomorrow!

I shall return to Michigan with so many stories never before mentioned, so many photos never before seen, and so many memories that will never be forgotten.

There have been over 900 bodies sent to the morgue here from Katrina, and more continue to come in from the New Orleans area.

I came upon an abandoned hearse on a deserted road but was unable to check the vehicle for a body. It is greatly assumed that there wasn't a body in it, but my curiosity will be forever unsated.

Out of the 400 horses that were at the Lamar-Dixon compound, 370 of them have already been claimed and picked up.

I have said my goodbyes, handed out cookies, and did one "final concert" on the piano (as it was requested of me), in my last days here.

I have used eight languages on this trip and I only speak six! However, I was able to converse in several more languages that I have been teaching myself, and that was just so amazing to be able to do so.

Never did I dream that would be possible, but it is so inspiring to have used so many valuable skills, all at the same time, and all in the pure desire to make a difference.

Here I am saying my last few goodbyes, and dreading the chill that Michigan has to offer and the snow soon to come. I have to return home quickly to run an election for Tyrone Township. They are counting on me.

Every volunteer much also out-process with a psychiatrist before they fly back home, and in my meeting with the psychiatrist on duty, she was at a loss for words. I'm sure she was used to people falling to pieces in front of her, needing strength and advice to pull it together before being able to return home after all the traumatic events down here, but not with me.

I was asked to share with her my 3-week journey here on the Operation, and she was so impressed with my accomplishments and refreshing take on how to effectively handle a recovery operation that she just commended me and said, "That is amazing, I can't believe someone your age has been able to do so much here, and with such a positive attitude. You are a very, very strong person." And then proceeded to sign me off as "ready to be released from duty".

I think I shall find it strange to return home though. I am leaving behind a "third-world country" status of hurricane-stricken Louisiana, a place where I had to wear a weapon, a place I couldn't trust most anyone, a place that was full of threats and dangers and people dying...to go back to a place where people are just enjoying normal life. Is that even right?

Should we be enjoying our life, while there are people just south of us struggling to survive? Homeless? Injured? Lost? Helpless? Burying their loved ones? It didn't seem right and it is with these thoughts that I will return to my home.

Sincerely,

-Rosie the Riveter

THE END

SUNDAY, OCTOBER 23rd
IN CLOSING
10:15 P.M.

Being down here, was the first time in my whole life that I was able to use ALL of my skills at once and to be on the frontlines of an operation in which I was able to see firsthand the impact of all that my hands touched.

It is with these words that I will close this diary. Take these stories and share them with someone you know. Take time out of your day to think about someone else that may need a moment of your time. It is never too late to make a difference.

Don't forget the important things in life, they aren't usually recognized until it is too late. Tell someone you love them, and show them love. Love truly is the strongest power on earth. Be the person you want to see in others. Act the way you want the world to be around you.

Never fear doing what's right. Never be scared of being the only one. You probably <u>will</u> be the <u>only one</u> in that moment. Just do it. Be you. There is no one else on earth that can be you. Everyone else is already taken. Live your life the way you always dreamed of living it. And most importantly live it for others.

-Rosie the Riveter

About the Author:
Ivy Stone

Ivy Stone is a well-respected author from Michigan in the United States. She speaks six languages and owns a Company that offers services in translating, interpreting and specialized instruction in multiple foreign languages. Foreign Five Company serves clients all throughout Michigan, the United States and Internationally.

For information on how to get her "Medical Spanish For Healthcare Professionals" Program into your hospital (to educate doctors and nurses on how to communicate with patients that only speak Spanish) email: foreignfive@yahoo.com.

Ivy began writing in her teens and published a cookbook at the age of 16. She loves helping others and doing relief work; publishing her first novel "Katrina Diary: What They Never Told you About Hurricane Katrina" in January of 2016.

Ivy has a second novel, a spy thriller, coming out in late 2016, which will also be made into a movie shortly after it's highly anticipated release.

Feel free to keep in touch by "liking" her page found at: **www.facebook.com/IvyStonePublishing**. She looks forward to hearing from her readers and keeping in touch with her fans from around the world.

Disclaimer: Please note that Ivy Stone is from Michigan in the United States, not to be confused with any other author or person who may have assumed her name.

www.ingramcontent.com/pod-product-compliance
Lightning Source LLC
Chambersburg PA
CBHW081203170426
43197CB00018B/2911